Examined
Lives

Roberta Reb Allen

ARCHWAY
PUBLISHING

Archway Publishing books may be ordered through booksellers or by contacting:

Archway Publishing
1663 Liberty Drive
Bloomington, IN 47403
www.archwaypublishing.com
1 (888) 242-5904

ISBN: 978-1-4808-6320-0 (sc)
ISBN: 978-1-4808-6319-4 (hc)
ISBN: 978-1-4808-6321-7 (e)

Library of Congress Control Number: 2018907031

Print information available on the last page.

Archway Publishing rev. date: 08/28/2018

To my parents
to whom I am grateful for the good
they were able to give me
and
to Christine and Ricks,
my anchors

Contents

Foreword

I first encountered the work of Dr. Walter Freeman many years ago when I was an undergraduate studying psychology. His lobotomy techniques were presented as a cautionary tale. I vividly remember the black-and-white photographs of a smiling man (I believe wearing a suit) about to plunge what looked like an ice pick into the brain of a seemingly happy (female) patient. My fellow classmates and I were shocked.

Case studies of people who had received accidental brain injuries have long been a teaching tool in the fields of neurology and neuropsychology, but here was a physician purposely inflicting a brain injury with the promise that a patient's life would improve. We all felt that something was just not right.

The gross negligence and racism of the Tuskegee Study had come to light several years earlier and had found its way into the curriculum. Freeman and Tuskegee swirled together creating a mix of horror and questions. Ultimately, these were intellectual questions far removed in time and place from the actual scenes of these travesties in the name of medicine and science.

Roberta Allen has given us a fuller context, a human context, for lobotomies. She addresses several important contextual questions: Who received the procedure? How did patients find their way to Freeman? What family dynamics helped propel patients to his practice? The most important question is, What were the consequences for the patients, their spouses, and their children? She also indirectly explores the question we asked many years later—how had Freeman gotten away with it for so long?

As we follow the unfolding of the life of Roberta's mother, we encounter a series of clinical tragedies. Her first episode of what sounds like postpartum depression occurred in New York City. There were many talented clinicians who most likely could have successfully treated her. Another episode occurred in Washington, DC, again, a center of psychoanalytic treatment, but these highly trained clinicians were not consulted.

The longer I practice, the more fascinated I am by the ability of families to find the right clinicians to support their families' dynamics but the wrong clinician for the family member experiencing difficulties. Roberta's father, though highly educated and aware of the world, managed to find a— well, let's just say it, a quack. We can assume Dr. Freeman's instant evaluation did not go beyond his knowing that Roberta's mother had had electroshock therapy. He certainly did not explore the question with her father: Why are the difficulties your wife is experiencing so distressing to you? Finally, however, a clinical hero emerges. At a sanitarium far away from the advanced clinical training of the large cities,

Roberta's mother encounters a psychiatrist who guided her back to independent functioning.

Most troubling is the issue of consent. How was the procedure explained by Freeman? How did Roberta's father explain the procedure to his wife? The book raises a chilling question: did Roberta's mother consent in a desperate effort to save her marriage and hold onto her children? If so, that is not consent; it is collusion.

Sadly, the book gives us a sense that the same family dynamics that led to a lobotomy also led to Roberta's not being recognized as a child who had lost her mother. Or for her mother to not be recognized as a woman who had lost her children. Roberta Allen has shared her journey of recognizing that she lost her mother and discovering the mother she never knew and the multiple forces that shaped her life. She also gives us the missing context for the lobotomies performed by Freeman and the long-term consequences for his patients and their families.

—R. Dennis Shelby, PhD
Chicago

Chapter 1

Why?

The unexamined life is not worth living.
—Socrates

My life has been messy. At times, it has been almost unbearably messy, and that has had a far-reaching impact on my life. I did not suffer unrelenting misery. I have many vivid memories of moments full of joyful abandon as we neighborhood kids ran through the small woods near our tract houses newly built after World War II pretending we were horses or were riding horses—black with blazes on their foreheads and palominos. I also had moments of comfortable calm losing myself in books about Freddie the Pig and Dorothy in Ozland.

But during the first twelve years of my life, I changed residences twelve times, attended seven schools including two schools in two of those years, and changed major caregivers eleven times. I was torn between two very different religions—Catholicism and Methodism—and had a mother who was "adjudged insane." Later in life, I suffered three major depressions.

I had my first bout of depression in my mid-forties. I was a very independent woman who was used to taking care of things myself and being on top of my game. Gradually, however, my world became filled with too much stress and uncertainty. My husband, a freelance writer, lost his clients during the recession of the early 1980s. As the months dragged on, he remained out of work, and we had to get by on my meager salary. He was a smoker; to save money on cigarettes, he was reduced to picking up previously smoked butts off the street. If his mother, unsolicited, had not sent us money each month, we could not have made our mortgage payments.

We eventually got new jobs; I moved from a very stressful position to one that did not require me to put in sixty hours a week. In addition, I had just gone through a skin cancer scare that proved not to be life threatening.

With pressures easing, our lives should have been relatively bright. They were not. My husband and I hit a rough time in our marriage, our two kids were beginning to explore greater independence with the inevitable conflicts that entailed, and I developed IBS, irritable bowel syndrome. The pain was excruciating, and it went undiagnosed through three hospitalizations. I began to sink into depression; I was afraid to fall asleep as I felt the need to watch over myself. Then I started crying uncontrollably. Some rational part of my brain told me that if I was crying, I should find something to cry about. I imagined myself as a little, lonely girl in a white dress like the ones my grandmother used to make for me, and I cried for her.

I got psychiatric help. I was prescribed an antidepressant at such high levels that it made my hands shake. I had talk-therapy sessions that focused on my mother. As I progressed, I dreamed that as an adult, I reached down from above and snatched my younger self from my mother's arms. I thought that I was undergoing what she had endured and that I was saving myself from her efforts to draw me into her world.

I eventually was able to go off the antidepressants, stop therapy, and return to an even keel. Although the IBS continued, I thought I was past needing to deal with my childhood. Then came the Christmas of 2011. My husband's smoking had caught up with him the year before. His pulmonary fibrosis was so bad that at the end, there were only wispy trails of tattered lung showing on his MRI. Rather than spending Christmas with my children, I decided to spend it alone on the rural farm to which I had moved. My fierce independence took over. I somehow felt that I was too much of a drag on others, a burden if I inserted myself in their lives.

It was a wrongheaded decision. My IBS was so painful that unable to sleep, I contemplated suicide. I envisioned placing a chair at the top of my driveway, bundling up, and sitting there until the cold put me into a deadly sleep. I called my brother in a panic. He called my neighbor and friend, who took me to a hospital. I signed myself in. Within a few days, I was in better shape and on medications that were helping me sleep and softening my pain. Friends gave me much-needed comfort and found for me an analyst and a psychiatrist they thought would be good fits.

With their professional help, I wanted to impose some order and sense on the confused fragments of memories I had of my childhood. I had lived all my life with snippets of mental videos that seemed random: going into another room to cry to stop my parents from arguing, being frightened by my mother's emotional response to the movie *Show Boat* and looking out the back window of the car my father was driving as he took me from my grandmother's home in Dubuque. These and many others would swirl in my mind, and I would feel like the ball in a pinball machine ricocheting from one side to the other. I wanted to know not only where and when but as much of why as I could fathom.

Unlike my earlier analysis, I now had an abundance of resources I could draw from and a more focused path. My family members on both sides were loath to throw things out. I had hundreds of family letters, some dating to 1894. I had my mother's diary and scrapbooks she kept as a young girl and woman. I had my father's poetry and the novel he wrote later in life based on his experiences during World War II. All these gradually came into my and my brother's possession on the deaths of my mother, father, and grandmother.

I also had my brother Ricks, four years younger than me, who was unable to recall anything about his early days or about our mother until—as he

remembered—he met her for the first time when he was ten. Even so, he was able to provide valuable points of view as well as pieces of information he had gleaned from conversations with those involved. My psychiatrist and my analyst also provided important perspectives on what I uncovered and helped me confront it.

Finally, being a historian by nature and training, I am a dogged and meticulous researcher who is able to ferret out additional documents and information, including what remained of my mother's patient records in Walter Freeman's files and at the Independence Mental Health Institute to which she was committed. Some of my research led to dead ends. Documents, particularly many medical records, had been destroyed. I would dearly love to have them as they would have helped answer some of the questions that remain. I found enough, however, to piece together an understanding of what had occurred during my childhood.

So my journey of discovery began in which I learned hard and surprising truths or as close to truths as I could get. Of course when I started, I already had images of my parents I had formed over the years. I thought I knew my father better as I had spent more of my grade school and high school years with him. To my mind, he was a good guy, a glad-hander able to get along well with almost anyone, unpretentious, and optimistic almost to a fault. He threw himself heart and soul into his work, so he was not always around much on weekdays. But on the weekends, he made time for us kids. We played various sports (tennis was his favorite) or went on long car rides. He loved history and celebrating Easter and

Christmas. He supported me in whatever I did, but he did not in the end really understand me or consider my feelings. He was given to making decisions quickly and following his personal dreams regardless of their impact on his family.

My mother was pleasant, kind and devoted to her religion but not very sophisticated. She seemed to care little for reading or any intellectual pursuits. She was not nearly as interesting as my father, and the love she expressed for me at times seemed almost smothering. These images I had were to dramatically change and become much more complex as I examined their lives.

Chapter 2

On to Chicago—Gretchen

My parents, Gretchen Richard and Everett Reb, met in Chicago. My mother's scrapbooks from her time there introduced me to a woman I had never met before. She had quit college in Dubuque, Iowa, an old river boat city on the Mississippi River, and made the four-hour train ride to a more exciting and glamorous life in the big Midwestern city she had visited many times before.

She arrived in Chicago in June 1937 on her twentieth birthday. The first thing she and her friends did was to take a speedboat ride on the Chicago River. The next day, she and her best friend got jobs waitressing at a party for the prizefighter Jack Dempsey.

Gretchen was hardly the first young single woman attracted to city life. With the gains of the early women's movement including the right to vote and the loosening of old social mores during the 1920s, it was no longer considered improper for young women to be out on their own. They usually lived together, perhaps in residential apartment buildings housing only women. In fact, Gretchen's Aunt Martha, who worked as a millineress on North Michigan Avenue, had preceded her to Chicago.

Gretchen took up residence and worked in the area around North Michigan Avenue—Rush Street, Oak Street, and Chicago Avenue were her haunts. It was a lively, posh part of town then and still is. Water Tower Place stands where one of the apartment houses she lived in had stood.

Gretchen was ambitious, very good at what she did, and ready to devour the good times Chicago offered. Her first position was as a waitress at the Walgreens Drug Store at Rush and Oak Streets. In those days, the Walgreens stores had long lunch counters along one wall with stools for patrons. This Walgreens had an extensive menu, serving breakfast, lunch, and dinner

and offering as dinner drinks a choice of domestic port, sherry, muscatel wine, fruit juice, or chilled tomato juice. My mother commented in her scrapbook "Came to work here September 1937. Liked it right away as it was glamorous ... it is one of the busiest little Drug Stores I have ever seen sometimes we serve 1000 people a day." She eventually worked her way up to be night manager.

There, Gretchen met and charmed many patrons. They included forty-eight-year-old Joe, a taxi driver who brought her flowers—"Just a friend. But a sweet one" she wrote. Many of the patrons who knew her by name were entertainers

(dancers, piano players, etc.) at the many restaurants, lounges, and bars in the area. There was Al, the former owner of the Granada Gardens where well-known orchestras of the era such as Guy Lombardo's got their starts. "He has been a millionaire twice and lost it both. Hasn't make a nickel in 4 years but still drives a big LaSalle and leaves quarter tips [pretty good for

those days]." Lita Chaplin, Charley Chaplin's former wife, would drop in at night.

After eight months, she moved on and up to become head receptionist for almost two years at the Younkers Café at 51 East Chicago. "During this time I lived and learned and had lots of fun." She managed twelve waitresses including Ruth, "a sad piece of humanity who was a street walker on the side."

Gretchen was the darling of the Younkers, father Edward and son Richard. When she started, Edward was in charge, and she got as a Christmas bonus a round-trip ticket to Dubuque to be with her parents for the holidays.

The next Christmas, Richard was in charge and gave her "a glamorous nightgown or dressing gown." There is no indication of any romance between them that such a gift might suggest, and Gretchen certainly would have mentioned it in her scrapbooks as she mentioned so many other men she went out with. In fact, it was older Edward, who already had a "grand person" for a girlfriend, who gave my mother one of the most exciting, romantic days of her life. "It was his good-bye gift [before he turned the restaurant over to his son]. I think he is an excellent example of a perfect employer." On the back of the lunch menu she saved from that day, she wrote this rapturous account.

> Mother's Day, May 13—Happiest day of my life— flying to Racine [Wisconsin] with Eddie—The way he touseled [*sic*] my hair—the rich fertile fields like a patchwork quilt, the sun setting in a glow of red. The clouds in the sky, the tiny houses, the worthlessness of worry. The

freedom of the birds—Landing at the Municipal air field, following Eddie like a little puppy, eating lunch and the fat waitress. Walking in and out talking to the aviators of the airliners, feeling important cause we were allowed in the field. His nonchalance with my hair very wild, all the people he knew, Al Jolson being paged [a singer famous at the time for singing songs like "Dixie" in blackface], crowds watching air liners and us, flying back at nite [*sic*]. The tiny jeweled city and Eddie's hand on my back to steady me. The landing in a 'black whole [*sic, hole*]'—a scotch and soda, music, missing the train and our personal feeling—His leaving the restaurant and his honesty even though it hurt [my mother may have had a "crush" on him which he scotched]—my resolution.

On the front of the menu, she exclaimed, "from 5:30 till 1:30—Paradis, Heaven, I must have dreamed it." He gave her words of advice that she dutifully wrote down and resolved to remember: "Fools rush in where angels fear to tread" and "Immorality may be fun but it's not fun enough to take the place of 100% virtue and three square meals a day."

Gretchen left Younker's in May 1941 to take a position as hostess or, as she was called, room captain at the Camellia House at the swanky Drake Hotel. This was the top of the ladder in her field. Gretchen called it "a dream come true." The individual responsible for hiring her obviously thought highly of her. Gretchen had applied for a position in April, but before hearing from them, she visited her folks in Dubuque.

She received an airmail letter there from the Drake: "Really need a hostess immediately but, seeing that you left Chicago before I was able to contact you, will hold the position for you until 2 o'clock Friday, April 25th. Will be unable to hold it any longer so hope I can count on you being here at that date and time." She was.

It was a glamorous job. "We have such people as guests as ... Clark Gable, Joan Blondell, Greta Garbo, ... Harold Lloyd ... and far more celebrities." At the time, there was a glossy weekly news gazette that was a who's who of the socially prominent from around the world who visited Chicago and frequented the Drake. The June 14, 1941 edition mentioned among others Supreme Court Justice William Douglas and his wife, a former assistant conductor of the Chicago Symphony, the foreign minister for the Netherlands Legation, and Jinx Falkenberg, a young movie star of the time.

Major business banquets were a weekly affair. On New Year's Eve in 1942, Arthur Wirtz, owner of the Detroit Red Wings and later the Chicago Blackhawks hockey teams, and his wife gave a bash at which the famous Olympic ice skater Sonja Henie, whose shows Wirtz produced, appeared with the cast of the 1943 Ice Review. On the menu were stuffed ostrich egg capers and filet mignon.

Although she loved Chicago, Gretchen maintained her connections with her family; she entertained them in Chicago, visited them at Christmas, went with them on an extended vacation to the Black Hills, and visited Tanglewood, her grandfather's fishing camp near Fergus Falls, Minnesota.

When her father became ill in May 1939, she went back to Dubuque to help out. She had a major bone of contention with her father over her smoking, something I am sure she saw as sophisticated. Her father offered her $100 (almost $1,500 in today's money) if she would stop smoking for a year. She did not take him up on the offer.

While on the job, Gretchen was all business. In fact, she got a complaining note from one of her swains who had dropped in where she was working just to say hello: "I concentrated upon catching your eye in the hopes that you might bend one inch from strictly business and give me a quick flicker of a smile and maybe say 'Hello' back at me. All very, very businesslike, to be sure."

Outside of work was quite a different matter. She enjoyed Chicago to the full. She was artistic and took two terms at the American Academy of Art, where among other classes she studied fashion illustration. In those days, newspapers generally used illustrations instead of photographs for clothing ads.

She belonged to a theater group she referred to as "bohemian"; she played a minor role in a production they did of Richard Sheridan's *School for Scandal.* Judge Caplan, one of her patrons, gave her passes to different theaters. She heard the famous violinist Mischa Elman at the Auditorium Theatre, and she saw John Barrymore in the play *My Dear Children* at the Selwyn Theater and Lillian Gish in Clarence Day's *Life with Father* at the Blackstone Theatre.

Gretchen must have hardly lived in her apartment. She was attractive, gregarious, full of energy, and fun loving. In her scrapbook are many comments about her seemingly endless visits to restaurants, nightclubs, and bars in downtown Chicago; the word *fun* was used constantly. She went out with relatives and friends from Dubuque and groups of Chicago friends, and she went on double and single dates. She had scores of boyfriends and would-be boyfriends whom she candidly commented on in her scrapbooks. These included Harry, "Northwestern dental student nice fellow"; Bob, "who is studying to be a doctor. He is too old"; Jim, "Very charming in a boring way, too stiff, too English"; another Bob, "Had lot of fun together. He had a hearty zest for life"; and Earl, "Had some grand times with Earl."

There were also others with whom she had more-sustained relationships and about whom she commented more fully, including Jack,

> the gym instructor at the Lawson YMCA who I saw Chicago with for awhile [*sic*].

He is one of the most intelligent men I ever met. Looks like Errol Flynn and reminds you of Rett [*sic*] Butler in "Gone with the Wind"— He reminds you of a knight in the times of "Round Tables" and swords. We took in one nite [*sic*]—the "Dome" of the Sherman, "Rickett's," "Ye Old Cellar," "Old Heidelburg," "Adolfo's," "Augustino's" and the "Blue Star." We also played ping pong—fought and walked a lot. He is 24 years old and has an exceptional esprit.

With Jerry, she visited "The Ranch ... afterward on the way home Jerry and I spied a baby buggy in an apartment house hall and we stole it and I rode down Rush Street in a baby buggy. Fun. They took the buggy back though."

The next day, Jerry sent her a note with an ad for a baby buggy: "You must have been a beautiful Baby—you still are you darlin' dope." She described him as "a big Irish good-natured and light hearted fellow who I had grand times with." He, however, was more serious about her. "One Sunday morning a proposal of marriage at the door. Jerry surprised me on way to church—by meeting me at the door and proposing." She obviously turned him down.

Gretchen definitely brought out the giddiness in men. While waiting for her to dress for a New Year's Eve date, an old friend from Dubuque typed her a note: "Gretchen Richard is nuts and I don't mean maybe, signed, sealed and delivered on this New Year's eve, A.D. 1937 ... The world's prize sap—am I ever, look at what I'm going out with tonite [*sic*]. Heaven preserve me from the wiles of this wicked woman."

While she was in Dubuque looking after her father, a friend who was a cabbie by night and a musician and collector of old song sheets by day wrote her hoping that her father would get back to full health.

> Principally, of course we wish that for your sake, but even so it goes much further than that. You are a good advertisement for your parents Gretchen and apart from their love for you, they have a right to be proud of you as well, which is a blessing that many worthy couples do not always cash in on. Some children become songwriters [himself], others become lovely little imps like yourself. While I personally wouldn't know, but I've excellent reasons for believing that there is something about the institution of being a "nice" person that yields enormous pleasure and satisfaction in so being. Frankly I doubt in all sincerity that there is a satisfactory or synthetic substitute quite as good ... All of us in Chicago, Susie [a nickname], who know you, love you, because we feel that you are just such a gal. That is the secret of our admiration for you. You seem to us to be the sort of person we would proudly hail as our future daughter, sweetheart and friend, and I know we always will be.

But "nice" as Gretchen was, she could be scornful. Ted took her to a dance at the Chicago Stadium that the Federation of Musicians was giving in honor of Edward J. Kelly, "the best mayor Chicago ever had." Next to the card accompanying a Valentine's Day gift, she wrote, "Orchid from Ted, but late." By Christmas, she referred to him as "a was been." Sam, miffed at Gretchen's choosing other dates over him, wrote her a letter breaking off their relationship: "You can do as you please. So I'll say thanks for a swell ride on a merry go round." Her comment on this was, "The futility of life or same thing of course I mean Sam's."

Gretchen also had a temper and got into fights with various girlfriends and boyfriends. While on a visit to Dubuque, she went to a dance with a high school heartthrob, but he incurred her ire when he did not respond to the letter she sent him. He responded. Following a fight she had with a long-term boyfriend, he wrote her,

> As I am definitely not a big enough man to face you, I am going to try and cleanse my conscience by telling all, from the very first I wanted to marry you and this is one thing I do mean Gretchen, when I say I wanted to marry you. I see now where I went about it the wrong way, but we will skip all that, but what I do want to confess is this Gretchen, is that towards the end when I wanted you so, I selfishly invented things in my mind thinking that I could win you that way, well, I was wrong, darn good and wrong.

Later in the letter, he accused her of cruelty.

> Gretchen your [sic] cruel through and through, It is not just my thoughts but several others, I don't know whether you mean to hurt people, you probably don't but the fact still remains that you do, Gretchen, I am sorry that I made

a damn fool out of myself, all I can say is that I thank the Lord in Heaven, that I did make you angry at me ... You hurt others, some day Gretchen, you are going to meet some fellow you really do care for, and you are going to ruin it, because Gretchen were [*sic*] all human, even Christ himself, had temptations, some conquer the others don't, but even worse Gretchen than weakening and submitting to your temptations, is being unable to forgive the transgressions, of others ... Gretch, when I asked you to forgive me, I didn't mean to go with you again, all I wanted was just a little forgiveness, ... but you were cruel and wouldn't, don't think Gretchen it is just me that your [*sic*] cruel to, everyone, I know, well laugh Gretchen if it makes you feel good, but I know that you can't laugh and smile to [*sic*]. I am sorry you are like you are, because you have so many good points. I am sorry I bored you so long, take it easy kid, or its [*sic*] going to be darn good and tough.

Presumably, this swain made some sexual advances Gretchen had not appreciated, but she wrote next to the copy of the letter, "He is a lot of fun and we made up after the fight." He "has a marvelous opera voice but does bookkeeping [for a living]. He has a marvelous personality and always makes everybody laugh."

The same issue of inappropriate sexual advances seems to lie at the heart of a letter she received in April 1940 from another boyfriend, who was "a fine lawyer—who also was going to Law School. He lived in Beverly Hills and had very nice people (parents)." She went with him for eight months. "He was a fine Catholic."

Then something happened that led to this missive from him.

> Dear Teddy [a nickname], I am still the confused young man about everything. I was lost Saturday night [when] I said goodbye to you at 721 Rush St. I am sorry about this afternoon. I know you will be allright [*sic*] and happy were [where?] you out [are?] now. I hope you will never be as unhappy and on as moving ground as I am now. I have the feeling I just want to be alone and not make you any more as unhappy as I have. I am convinced you will be better off without me. I will not be up this weekend or for some time. Fondly Bye and God bless you.

Gretchen wrote about the situation to a good friend from high school and received this reply.

> Got your letter. Was awfully glad to hear about the old fashioned girl angle. It's so easy to go ahead and do what [the boyfriend] wanted you to. He probably thinks a hell of a lot more of you if he's any kind of a man at all—Irish or otherwise. Your Mother was telling me about Dr. Rueben [*sic*, Rubin, a dentist my mother had brought home for a weekend] She said he's very nice. You sound so much older and so much wiser Gretch and that sadness you probably

feel will make a much better person of you—
real and deep with a depth that will help you
understand other people ... I miss you so very
much, Gretch, as I always said there never was
anybody like you—whatever you did you were
honest ... Keep the old head up, Gretch, you
never were the type anybody could get down
too much spirit I always said.

The ex-boyfriend later became a friend again but never in
another relationship with Gretchen.

This is the woman my father married and the mother I
never knew. Going through her diary and scrapbooks was a
revelation to my brother and me. But by the time we were old
enough to really interact with her, her sparkle and drive had
been taken from her.

Chapter 3

On to Chicago—Everett

Everett arrived in Chicago in September 1940 to attend graduate school at Northwestern University's Medill School of Journalism. He had been inspired to take up a career in journalism by fellow Kansan William Allen White, a crusading small-town newspaper publisher who had gained a national reputation for his progressive stances against the Ku Klux Klan and his support for aiding the Allies before the United States entered World War II. White won the 1923 Pulitzer Prize for an editorial advocating free speech.

Everett, like Gretchen, was ambitious and looking to make a mark for himself. He came from a farming family that had moved to the small college town of Baldwin City, Kansas, so he and his sister Christine could attend Baker College, now Baker University, a private Methodist institution of higher learning. They both lived at home and worked part-time to put themselves through college, in each instance mainly by working in the college library.

I do not have anything equivalent to Gretchen's scrapbooks and diary for Everett. I do, however, have family letters that give some idea of his college life. Methodist though it was, Baker allowed sororities and fraternities as well as dances. My father had girlfriends—how many I do not know—and went on dates to dances, football games, and other campus events as well as meals at each other's houses. But he had no experiences quite like Gretchen's. She was far more worldly—no drinking, smoking, or nightclubs in Baldwin.

The tone of his letters to his sister Christine, who was doing graduate work at the University of Illinois at Urbana-Champaign when he entered college, is jaunty and upbeat much in keeping with the face he presented to the world the rest of his life. He had a saying: "As you go through life, brother/ whatever may be your goal/ keep your eyes upon the doughnut/and not upon the hole."

Things really have been happening today. I went to French at nine and found a bunch of students around the campus with paddles keeping everybody from going to class. They were enforcing a holiday because Baker took the football championship, or tied it. You can't imagine the school spirit that has been shown this year. At the Ottawa game to which I went, the students just about went mad. They tore down the goal posts, went down town, got together in groups in different cafes. I was in the Foote Coffee Shop, and yelled and shouted themselves hoarse. It surely was fun. Boy, I yelled so much at the game I couldn't speak and I could barely move, my knees were so weak ... Well, to get back to this holiday [Thanksgiving], which happened to be on my birthday what a coincidence the president ... would acknowledge it as a holiday. But the students went right on. Everybody got together at noon and had a big dinner, and then in the afternoon we had a free show—wild western. And all this time, Profs. were meeting their hypothetical classes, sending in absences which means double cuts. Prof. Gess lectured, it is said, just like the class was really there.

Everett was very involved in campus life; he played varsity tennis, basketball, and football, getting a broken nose for his trouble. By the time he graduated, he was treasurer of his senior class, head of the yearbook staff, and editor of the school newspaper.

The collection of his poetry written between 1937 and 1939 while he was in college, however, reveals an obvious darkness in his emotional life. He had hoped one day to publish the collection under the title *Smoke Bent on the Wind*. In fact, two of his poems were published in 1939 in a hefty volume called *The Yearbook of Modern Poetry*.

The themes of most of his poems—loneliness, death and love—were standard fare for aspiring poets of his age. But these themes so pervaded his work and seemed to penetrate him so deeply that for me, they are in stark contrast to his public persona. He wrote of his isolation and loneliness: "Far down the lonely road walk I/Just me, the wind, and the stormy sky/And I'll walk that road until I die/On the lonely road," "Despair like a haunted thing has crept into my heart," "Fall leaves cover my sorrow," "My brain is twisted tight with pain."

His poems on death do not seem mere poetic fodder but reflections of his encounters with the possibility of death. In the spring of his freshman year, he contracted scarlet fever, a bacterial infection involving a rash, sore throat, and fever. Today, it is treated with antibiotics, but there were none at that time. The disease developed into rheumatic fever and caused some scarring of his heart. While neither he nor his mother made a great deal out of the illness at the time, it was something that hung over him for the rest of his life and may have led to his poem "I saw death standing at the door." Death, however, declined to come in just yet.

In addition, he appeared to have had a girlfriend who died. He never mentioned this to me or my brother, nor are any such deaths mentioned in family correspondence, but his poems about her are obviously reactions to a very real situation. In one he agonized over being made to wait outside where she was being treated and pleaded "Dear God oh, please don't let her die."

Then a few years later, he penned this poem.

Tombstone, you lie
She did not die.
How dare you state so boldly
How dare you state so coldly
That she is dead.
She is as alive as screams
She is as alive as dreams
As laughter, as tears,
As loves, as years
Tombstone, you lie
She did not die
It was I.

The majority of his poems, however, deal not surprisingly with love. While he wrote some lyrical poems ("Bright golden threads of sunbeams in her hair," "Sweet lay your lips on mine"), most of these poems reveal major disappointments. And as the years passed, the poems on love became more detached and cynical. In 1939, just as he was graduating, he wrote,

My love was like a rose
One rose so delicately made
I dared not touch for fear that I
Might bruise it with my clumsy hand
And cause it then to die.
How jealously I kept that rose
That no one else should harm
The soft, sweet pureness of its shape
Divest it of its charm.
And yet my rose began to fade
Alarmed, I frantic tried

27

To catch the petals ere they fell.
But, alas, my rose had died.
Many roses now have bloomed
To fade as just before
Except that now I merely laugh
And toss them on the floor.

*****

One touch of her fingertips
Could thrill me more than a thousand lips
But I dare not touch her
To touch her would be hell.
For afraid I am the thing I held
Would be a woman's shell
While she looked at me from a distant rafter
Her eyes empty with a dark, cold, bitter
laughter
With a dark, cold, bitter laughter.

Everett's nonchalance in the first poem seems like a cover for the hurt he obviously experienced in this relationship. It must have had special meaning for him as many years later he had it printed on an elaborate plaque. The second poem seems to speak of his despair of knowing and being known by the opposite sex.

These poems revealed to me a side of my father I had never known. They expressed deep-seated emotions he felt but did not display to the world. More such revelations were ahead in my researches.

After graduation from college, Everett wrote no more love poetry, not even for Gretchen. On arriving in Evanston, just to the north of Chicago, he stayed near Northwestern's campus on Sheridan Road in a large, otherwise empty house owned by a wealthy woman who wanted someone to housesit in exchange for rent. He received some scholarship money and was chosen to join Sigma Delta Chi (now called the Society of Professional Journalists), the journalistic equivalent of Phi Beta Kappa. He was very proud of his life membership.

At Northwestern, he was an assistant to one of the journalism professors and a reporter for the Northwestern alumni magazine. He completed twenty-five hours toward his professional degree and needed just fifteen more when he left. I do not know why he left. From comments he made later to me, he had expected to return to finish the program. It may have been for lack of money, or perhaps he wanted to get out into the world and use his talents.

In April 1941, he moved to Chicago and had a brief stint as a short-order cook. That was soon followed by a job in his field—working for Chicago Club Magazines, which he described as "publishers of slick magazines for clubs and organizations." He also did public relations for the Lake Shore Club.

Everett rented a room in a Rush Street house occupied by a couple called the Glotfelty's. The Great Depression was still lingering, and people often took in boarders to help make ends meet. It so happened that at that time Gretchen lived in one of the other rooms there. So presumably, this is where they first met although there do not appear to have been any sparks at first.

In her scrapbook, Gretchen commented, "Attended [an event] with Everett Reb: a <u>plenty</u> nice boy that occupies the front room at our (Glotfelty's) house, me in back room." Her scrapbooks do not mention my father again until about the time they married, but a photo from August 1941 shows them together in front of their residence with my father quite adoring. Gretchen's mother thought they had known each other only for three months prior to their marriage; perhaps that was how long she had been aware of their dating.

Chapter 4

The Marriage

Gretchen and Everett were married on February 5, 1942, by a justice of the peace in Evanston, presumably at the city hall there. Gretchen did not wear a wedding dress but a tailored white suit she once showed me. She still had the by-then dried corsage pinned to it. She was twenty-four, and my father had just turned twenty-three at the time of their marriage.

Their parents were not present at the wedding. Everett's parents only learned of it afterwards. Gretchen's parents objected to a marriage outside the Catholic Church. Her mother thought the wedding had taken place at the stylish Maryland Hotel on Rush Street that boasted three hundred rooms, a restaurant, and a swinging dance club called the Cloister Inn, where the likes of Duke Ellington and Bing Crosby appeared. It seems likely that this was in fact where my parents spent their honeymoon evening and night.

It was an ill-fated match from the beginning as it involved the taut issues of religion and sex. Gretchen was a devout Catholic, and Everett came from a staunch Methodist background. Her mother later reported to officials at the mental institution to which Gretchen was admitted, "This couple had considerable difficulty in regard to their wedding plans. The parents [that is, my mother's parents] wanted them to come home and be married in the church and because of their religious differences, they did not want to." That was an understatement. Gretchen dutifully kept in a scrapbook the letter she received from her father disowning her. She and Everett had apparently agreed before they married that any children would be raised Catholic, but that they would not attend parochial schools.

Hers was not the Catholicism prevalent today after Vatican II. At that time, priests said Mass in Latin with their backs to the parishioners. It was more like watching a performance with the principal actor mumbling his words. Women had no upfront duties such as serving as readers or eucharistic ministers. They basically were responsible for keeping the fast day—Friday—when it was forbidden to eat meat as a token of sacrifice. Tuna fish casserole and macaroni and cheese were the menu items of the day. Nuns kept to their black habits and convents. Women did not enter a church bareheaded. It was forbidden to go to a Protestant service or read a Protestant Bible.

Gretchen's diary, which she kept from June 1932, when she turned fifteen, to April 1936, when she was almost nineteen and a year away from going to Chicago, reveals the strong appeal of the church for her; she belonged to pious church organizations such as the Catholic Daughters of America. In February 1933, she wrote,

Went to Church. Gee it seems go[ing] to be pious again diary: I love to say the stations diary [In saying the Stations of the Cross, the devout say prayers and meditate at each of the 14 different stations—usually on the side walls of a Catholic church—which depict Christ's last day on earth] but I'll only tell that to you (it's our secret).

Each year, the Catholic school she attended had a school retreat around Easter that involved devoting time to prayerful silence.

Went on Retreat diary, you know I really would like to keep the silence ones but nobody else does so I feel dumb keeping it!! ... We have a nice retreat master, he's really holy—I think I shall always remember the way his hands would protect the crucifix which he would handle while talking.

The next day, she reported, "My knees hurt from kneeling."

My Jesus, Mercy!

Everett was never a strict Methodist, but his parents were, and particularly his father, Louis. They came from the evangelical tradition of their youth and young adulthood. Aside from doctrinal differences with Catholicism, there were for want of a better term lifestyle, or from the Methodist point of view, moral differences with Catholicism. No drinking, no smoking, no playing cards, no working on Sunday.

Everett's sister, my aunt Christine, recalled that she and Everett did play games on Sunday but that the curtains had to be drawn to keep any neighbors from peering in. Everett's mother, Pearl, wryly reported to Christine in a letter, "We [she and Louis] were at church ... and ate dinner at Ellen's (very good) [Ellen's was a restaurant]. Dad was quite 'loathe' and made me do the paying (on acct. of Sunday), but he enjoyed the dinner."

I do not know what Pearl and Louis thought of the marriage at the time. Pearl visited Chicago and met Gretchen; the photograph of them together shows Pearl looking rather uncomfortable.

Not only were their religious backgrounds so different, but so had been their childhoods. Everett grew up on a farm in Frankfort, Kansas, near his Reb aunts and uncles, who farmed close by. In 1930, Frankfort had 1,346 people. When his family moved to Baldwin City, Kansas, the population was smaller—1,127. The family moved just as the Great Depression started. They eventually lost the farm in Frankfort, which they had not sold before moving, as well as the dairy farm the family had purchased outside Baldwin City.

Everett worked from an early age. He had to milk cows, a chore he did not relish. When as a little girl I was excited to learn about his farm experiences, he told me that as far as he was concerned, milk came from bottles. At age thirteen, he was a printer's devil, or apprentice, at a Kansas weekly newspaper print shop.

After the loss of the farm, his parents kept one cow from whose milk Pearl would make food items such as cottage cheese to sell to neighbors. She also prepared and sold dressed—plucked and cleaned—chickens from the chickens they raised. Louis did handiwork and was the local representative for the Starke Brothers nursery. Their financial situation was precarious. They received rent erratically from the people who were renting the farm in Frankfort before it was foreclosed. They also periodically received Louis's share of the proceeds from the sale of crops on the jointly owned family homestead back in Frankfort that an older brother managed.

Sometimes, one of Pearl's brothers sent them a small sum.
They also took in student
boarders from Baker
College. Concerns about
paying bills and penny-
pinching efforts were a
constant theme in Pearl's
correspondence with her
daughter, Christine. Pearl
would relate how much her
meals cost and the cost of
items of clothing purchased
down to the penny as well
as how she had altered
clothing to continue to

make it useful. The family was obviously resourceful but had
little money for frills.

It was not a happy family. Pearl
and Louis did not get along. Christine
told me that if divorce had not been
frowned upon at that time, Louis and
Pearl would surely have gotten one.
Pearl greatly favored Christine over
Everett and let him know it. He was not
emotionally close to his father either.
Sports were his passion and later he
could not recall that his parents ever
asked about his sporting activities or

attended games; his father never even played catch with him.

All of this had a devastating effect on Everett. In a letter written to Christine many years later, he bitterly recalled the moment, at age ten, that estranged him from his family.

> It happened when we lived at the Sixth St. house on a Sunday. We had just returned from church and were sitting in the front room. Mother was sitting on the piano bench with her ulcerated leg up and resting on it (I always felt guilty that I caused it when I was born). As she was wont to do upon occasion, she was giving Pop hell for having looked at some woman during the service, and announced that she was leaving. She said, 'I'm taking Christine with me.' Then she looked at me and said nothing. There was a long silence, and Pop finally said. 'I'll take him.' Something snapped in my brain, and I never felt a part of the family again. I felt unwanted and unloved.

So fighting was something that was ominous and hurtful for Everett. Emotional clashes were to be avoided.

In contrast, Gretchen grew up in a much larger city, Dubuque, which in 1930 had a population of 41,679. It was a livelier place than Baldwin City. Her parents got along fine. Many years later, after his death, Ida wrote on the back of a photograph of her husband in his wedding outfit, "my beloved Joe." They did, however, have different temperaments. My grandfather Joe was a very religious, soft-spoken man. My grandmother Ida, whom Ricks and I called Nana, was a rugged, practical woman. Her father had owned an eatery of sorts in Alton, Iowa, with a pool room in back, but he subsequently purchased a fishing camp in Fergus Falls, Minnesota. Nana and her sister would help their mother fix the group meals for lodgers in the summer.

She talked of taking her younger brother several miles to school in the winter with wolves howling in the distance. She was not afraid to drive a car long distances by herself, rather rare in her day. When the deadly flu epidemic struck after World War I, she took out a life insurance policy. She suffered the loss of several  children through miscarriages and an early death. My mother was her only surviving child.

Joe and Nana were from a social class similar to Pearl's and Louis's. Joe had been a mechanic on the railroad but lost his job during a strike. At the time of Gretchen and Everett's marriage, he was custodian at the Catholic girls' school Gretchen had attended. His income, however, was steady. According to the 1940 census, he earned $1,640 (about $28,000 in today's money). Nana may have supplemented that by doing seamstress work.

As I read Gretchen's diary, I got no idea of an economic depression going on except for her one statement when Roosevelt was elected: "Last night was election night and Roosevelt got it. I'm glad Diary maybe he'll help the poor people. I mean give them jobs." She showed no concerns about money. She went to the doctor as needed for orthopedic and dental work and a sinus condition. She would occasionally go shopping with her mother and get

new outfits. She took music and dancing lessons, and she became quite a good dancer. She earned some money after graduation from high school by performing at local venues with a partner.

And as she would subsequently have in Chicago, Gretchen had a rich social life with a large group of friends who were welcomed by her parents into their house. There were plenty of sleepovers. Gretchen went swimming, ice skating, to the movies (a lot), to dances and parties, to the fights, and to football games. She attended a carnival, a Shakespeare play, and a symphony concert, and she engaged in some innocent hijinks such as skipping school and climbing the fire escape there.

When she graduated from high school in 1935, she started taking night classes at the local Catholic women's college,

Clarke College, including classes in art, another one of her passions. But her activities continued much the same. She confided in her diary, "Diary Dear, I crave excitement."

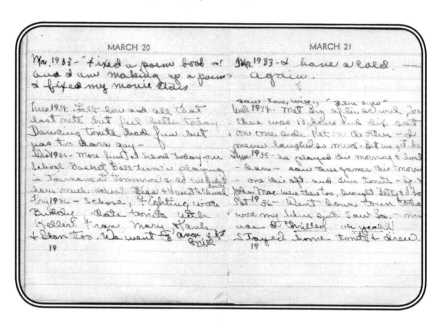

As was the case with Everett, she had strife in her life but nothing from which she recoiled. Her diary is full of instances of her getting mad at boyfriends, boyfriends getting mad at her, and her mother getting mad at her for allowing boys to stay too late at the house.

And Gretchen was not above getting into a fight with a nun. "Gee! I had fun but was she mad." But these emotional upheavals were taken as a regular part of life and do not appear to have been bitter. They were soon made up. No one seemed to remain irked with anyone for very long.

She appeared to have very good relations with her parents; she went with them together and individually to movies, to restaurants, on visits to relatives, and to Chicago. She went with her mother in 1933 to the World's Fair and with her father the next. Prohibition was still in effect when she went with her mother, who nevertheless took her to a speakeasy to sip gin. When she went with her father, she saw Barney Oldfield, the daredevil race car driver. "Gee I loved the tall buildings, the excitement."

I have wondered for a long time why my parents married. I believe that in a solid marriage, what you want and what you need have to be much the same. I do not think my parents asked those questions of themselves; I think they went with for want of a better term the spirit of the moment, not what they needed in the long run. Gretchen needed an exciting, romantic, Catholic spouse, and Everett needed a rather staid wife who would take care of a home for himself and his children.

Of course in the end, the question is not really answerable; what attracts two people is a matter of the heart. I can, however, speculate. Obviously, there was sexual attraction between them. They had interests in common. Both enjoyed sports; as mentioned earlier, Everett had played tennis and football in college, and Gretchen had played basketball and tennis and loved to swim and ice skate. Both loved poetry. Gretchen had written poetry in high school and even won a prize sponsored by Drake University. She also had copied out in bound books poetry to which she was drawn written by the likes of Sara Teasdale, Edna St. Vincent Millay, Dorothy Parker, Lord Byron, Wordsworth, and Countee Cullen. The latter surprised me as he was a major African-American poet of the Harlem Renaissance but not one with whom I would expect a young Catholic girl in Dubuque to have been familiar.

On Everett's side, I do not believe he had ever met a woman like my mother—so vivacious and much the free spirit. She was certainly not like his mother, who was a martyr to the cause of her foot sores and who worried about whether a print dress she had received was too loud to wear to church. Everett came from a far more repressed background and was probably dazzled by the possibility of Gretchen's offering him a liberating relationship, sexual and otherwise. One of the poems he wrote in college hints at this desire.

> That me that I appear to be
> Is not the me I fear to be
> I'd like to be so free, so free
> To live a life of liberty,
> In love, and life, and great desires
> In appetites and thirsts the fires
> My deep most urge to re-create
> My life and times upon my slate.

It is harder for me to imagine Gretchen's choosing my father out of all the men she dated. He was nice looking, but so were many of her other boyfriends. He was outgoing, ambitious, driven, and intelligent, which she would have admired. He may not have been as sexually aggressive as some of her other boyfriends, and she may have appreciated that.

Living in the same house with Everett may also have created an emotional intimacy that was almost family-like. Gretchen was obviously romantic, and she adored the Glotfelty's: "Two people against the storm of life who seemed to find complete happiness. I make my home with them ... are like a part of me." She may have believed that she and Everett could emulate the Glotfelty's and weather "the storm of life" including religious differences together.

Most certainly, the entry of the United States into World War II played a role in their decision to marry. Such an emotionally charged atmosphere spurred many a marriage. In fact, just shortly before their marriage, Everett was classified 1-A.

Her friends expressed some surprise at her marriage. A former boyfriend who was working in Detroit wrote ruefully to her in January,

> Was quite surprised to hear of your betrothal although the last time I saw you I thought it looked pretty thick. Especially when I left and you wouldn't kiss me in front of him. My! How times have changed. No kidding though, I think in a way you played me a dirty trick. Here's why. For years you and I have been running around together off and on. After all we had much in common. We both knew what was in each others [sic] hearts. And then after all this, after the many hours we spent together, you run off and marry some guy I don't even know, cheating me out of that long cherished chance, the chance to play the organ at somebody's wedding.

The marriage almost immediately had major tension. Years later, when I was in my forties and long after my mother's death, my father visited me. As he and I were taking a walk around my neighborhood, my father out of nowhere suddenly said, "You know your mother told me she was not a virgin on our wedding night."

I later found out that my father had confided the same to my brother. We don't know why he did that. Was he using it as a justification for eventually divorcing her? Was he looking for sympathy for the idea that our mother had deceived him into marriage? It hardly seemed like an appropriate subject to discuss with children no matter how old they were, and I did not pursue the topic further.

But with Gretchen, given the era in which she lived, women were expected to be virgins until they married. I do not know whether Everett was a virgin until he married Gretchen, but I suspect that was the case.

Over the years I thought a good deal about my father's revelation. Something did not ring true about it. While her scrapbooks show her to be obviously flirtatious and that she enjoyed eroticized environments, there is no evidence she had had sexual intercourse with anyone before she married my father. She went out for fun, but she had boundaries. When guys began to push her sexually, she resisted. She was a devout Catholic, which then and now preaches abstinence until marriage.

In addition, looking back at her Dubuque days, Gretchen's diary presents a very gregarious teenager with lots of friends and a series of boyfriends with whom she would fall in "love" only to move on to another infatuation in short order. She was also briefly in love with one of her girlfriends. The diary does not reveal her to be particularly sexually adventurous. As her diary starts out, she is interested in George until she went to her grandfather's fishing camp in July and met nineteen-year-old Joe, with whom she became enamored: "Went fishing with Joe (alone!?) (Joe can squeez [*sic*]). Joe is one keen kid ... We went to the dance tonight had a keen time (I said 'I didn't Gee)."

Back home, she missed him for a short while, but he started dropping out of the picture. In the middle of August, she wrote, "Right now I would love Joe, adore Tom, devour Vern, and be crazy about any other male." She had her first "date" in February 1933—a necking party. She crashed a party in November of the same year: "Did I ever get my full of necking. Virginia and S. were nuts. I had a nice time but got to[o] much petting." In April 1934: "Met new guy—a blonde fell so did I so we Xed (Gee diary—I bet he thinks I'm cheap.)" "Donald came down tonight [to her house]—I have a cold diary and he'll have a cold—yes twice."

As she got older, she became more circumspect. She wrote of two friends who were necking at her house, "I don't know maybe I'm nuts but I don't like it." She definitely did not like friends arriving on her doorstep "tight": "Was I sore. I guess I'm old fashioned." And "I'll never forget the 'wild party' on August 4. Gee were the girls tight and did I yell to come home—I was so disgusted. I guess I'm a wet blanket diary!!"

Then in 1935, the year she turned nineteen, she met someone nine months younger than she was whom she stuck with for almost a year with many an upheaval between them but also good times. "Couldn't study very well ... Met him this noon. I like him I think but I'm always thinking that. So what!" Then in May: "I don't care so much about going out any more—dam [him]" In July: "We had fun ducking each other, etc. I like [him] I think diary." He told her that he liked her in September, and in October, he "kissed me for the first time tonite [*sic*]." Theirs was obviously a very chaste romance.

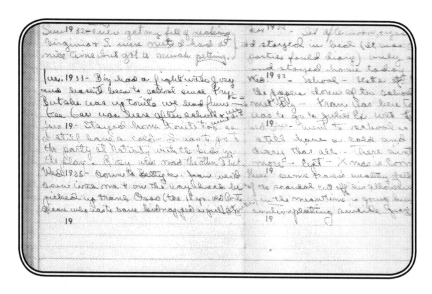

In January 1936, my mother wrote, "It was just a year ago—Gee I can't remember how it feels not being in love. Gee we sure have had fun doing little silly crazy things." I have wondered if my father did not remind Gretchen of this boyfriend she remembered fondly all her life.

But at the time, Gretchen was certainly not ready for marriage. She confided to her diary after this boyfriend had kissed her, "It was wonderful last nite [*sic*] and yet I think

I like money a little too much to get married." One of her college boyfriends told her he loved her ("tush, tush") and proposed in vain twice. "I wonder next year. I think I'll go to college—not here though—I want to go away acquire lots of poise, etc."

Thus it does not appear that my mother had gone much beyond kissing and necking. Petting is mentioned only twice in her diary.

So what exactly had my mother told my father? My father wrote his bitter letter to Christine in 1991, when he was at the lowest ebb in his life. He was in debt, living in a trailer in an isolated area of New Mexico where he had planned to grow pistachio trees and write his novel about World War II. He had not bothered to check whether there were available water sources for his trees. In his self-pity he recounted, "My sorrows with her [Gretchen] started three days after we were married when she told me, after claiming as a Catholic to be a virgin, that she had had a venereal disease. This was confirmed later by her mother, who claimed she got it from a toilet seat. Ha!"

My mother was eleven years old when she was diagnosed with gonorrhea. Of course we now know that contracting gonorrhea from a toilet seat is sheer nonsense, but that was the uncritical belief of the medical community at the time. It had not been based on scientific evidence. No one asked if what they were saying could have been proven. Doctors in the nineteenth century generally believed that the venereal diseases with which they were familiar, basically syphilis and gonorrhea, were spread through sexual intercourse by prostitutes. The children they encountered with gonorrhea were mainly from poor families in which the children claimed sexual assault, usually by their fathers.

As better means of detecting the disease appeared, doctors discovered to their consternation that it was not just poor children who contracted the disease but children from every walk of life. By the late 1920s, as better statistics were collected, 10 percent of the reported cases of gonorrhea involved girls under age thirteen.[1]

How could girls from "respectable" middle-class and upper middle-class families have gotten the disease? Health officials were loath to point the finger at the children's male relatives, who after all were considered fine, upstanding individuals. So although the medical community knew that the bacteria that causes gonorrhea dies quickly when exposed to air, they argued without one iota of proof that the lining of a young girl's vagina was so thin that it allowed possible infection from soiled objects such as toilet seats. This belief carried into the 1940s until after the introduction of the antibiotic sulfanilamide as an effective treatment.[2]

Had Gretchen actually contracted gonorrhea? Because most likely no test was done for the disease,[3] we do not actually know. The diagnosis would probably have been made based on signs such as a vaginal discharge, itching in the genital area, and burning when urinating. The uncertainty here is significant as Gretchen subsequently exhibited none of the typical signs of young girls who had suffered sexual abuse. Her diary does not reveal any sexual promiscuity, lack of self-esteem, depression, anxiety, or behavioral problems.[4]

(It is, however, true that childhood sexual abuse can have long-term effects and be associated later in life with anxiety and marital problems,[5] which my mother did experience.)

So I asked myself if there were another sexually transmitted disease with similar symptoms that could be spread without penetration having taken place. It is only since the 1970s that the medical world has identified many STDs, and there is one that can be contracted through genital touching—trichomoniasis. In fact, a specialist in gynecology I consulted indicated it could be spread through soiled linens. In an interview at the state mental institution, Gretchen revealed that she had had sexual relationships with girls on two or three occasions in "grade school or [*sic*, should be "and"] high school" and had engaged in mutual masturbation in Chicago, but she did not specify male or female. If mutual manipulation of genitals had been involved in her relationships with girls in grade school and one of them had been infected with trichomoniasis, that could have resulted in her contracting it. In such a scenario, there would have been no sexual abuse.

My brother and I have tried to figure out who would have sexually abused her if she did have gonorrhea. We do not believe it was her father for several reasons. He had not served during World War I, so there was no possibility of his having contracted gonorrhea from overseas encounters with prostitutes, and Nana would certainly never have tolerated any errant ways at home. And Gretchen seemed to have a positive relationship with her father. Her abuser, if she had been sexually abused, could have been a male relative, a high school or college student, a priest, or a stranger. In that event, it appears to have been of short duration as she did not contract gonorrhea again. More telling perhaps is the fact that she made no mention of such an incident in her statements to the mental health institute staff while frankly discussing other aspects of her sexuality.

But why had the issue about venereal disease even come up? As a good Catholic was my mother confessing so that there would be no secrets between them? Did she expect him to accept the revelation with compassion and understanding out of love for her? He certainly did not.

When I read my father's letter I was incredulous and angry. My mother had been eleven years old! Did he think she had spent her young life sleeping around? When he wrote the letter to Christine he was seventy-three years old and he was roughly that age when he made his revelation to Ricks and me. By that time it was well-known what a child's having gonorrhea implied. Did he deliberately not know? My father was given to seeing and hearing what he wanted to see and hear. He admitted to Christine that "Gretchen did offer me a chance to leave her, but I was too naïve to do it." Naïve about what? Himself? It all has the overtones of a Thomas Hardy novel.

Everett did apologize to Christine for his "temper tantrums," and she responded to his plight by helping him out financially, not by further recriminations. That was her nature.

It was my father's nature to hold deep and long-lasting grudges, as irrational as they might be. My brother told of a visit with my father to the old family homestead in Kansas where they spent an afternoon with my father's cousin. My brother found the cousin to be a gentle, antiquated soul. On leaving, Ricks commented on how he rather liked the cousin, and my father burst into a tirade about how the cousin had refused to share a sled with him when they were children. Another sled features in his letter to Christine as he revealed how upset he was that as children she got a new one and he got the hand-me-down. Shades of *Citizen Kane*.

At least in the short term, however, the wedding-night confession did not seem to affect their relationship. Not waiting to be drafted, Everett enlisted in the army at Camp Grant, Illinois, on March 4, a mere month after his marriage. In April, he was stationed at Scott Field, also in Illinois. He was a private in the 561st Technical School Squadron (Special) Air Corps; at the time, the air force did not yet exist as a separate branch of the military.

He trained at the Radio Operators and Technician School. Gretchen of course stayed in Chicago and continued working at the Drake. Scott Field was in downstate Illinois, about a four-and-a-half-hour trip. Gretchen would visit him, but obviously, the newlyweds saw little of each other throughout the early months of their marriage though they looked obviously happy in pictures from that time.

From the nature of his training, it is clear that Everett's role would have involved flying (he had actually hoped to be a pilot), but his high blood pressure, which he had inherited from his mother, put an end to that dream; high altitudes exacerbate hypertension.

In November 1942, he had his condition evaluated in a military hospital. The doctors hoped that resting for a few days might bring his blood pressure down to acceptable levels. Unfortunately, it did not, so Everett was honorably discharged just before Christmas. That must have been a bitter disappointment—hardly something that would have boosted his morale. But he was determined to serve in some capacity rather than be left behind. Almost immediately, he went by himself to New York to look for a job as a war correspondent, another romantic occupation like being a pilot, but one for which he was trained.

Chapter 5

On to New York City and My Birth

By January 30, 1943, Everett had landed a job with the Office of War Information through the auspices of Robert Rand, a colleague from Northwestern, who eventually died on a mission in Burma. At my mother's suggestion, I was named after him.

The Office of War Information was engaged in producing propaganda and conducting psychological warfare. The means available at the time were printed materials and radio transmissions. The goal was to maintain Allied morale and weaken that of the enemy. This type of "warfare" was relatively new, and some in Congress and the general public were suspicious of it as somehow not fair and un-American.[6] Everett worked as a news editor in the Overseas Operations Branch, Cable-Wireless (Radio) Section providing news to the troops.

He apparently first lived in the William Sloan House, a very large residential YMCA facility. It provided housing for over fifteen hundred servicemen. As a recently discharged soldier, he would have been welcomed. I say "apparently" because my father wrote a poem on their stationery.

The poem is startling. It reveals a marked change in attitude toward Gretchen. The poem is full of strikeouts and substitutions as if having been done in a highly emotional state, but the first two lines are clear: "I could love her, adore her/But instead I abhor her."

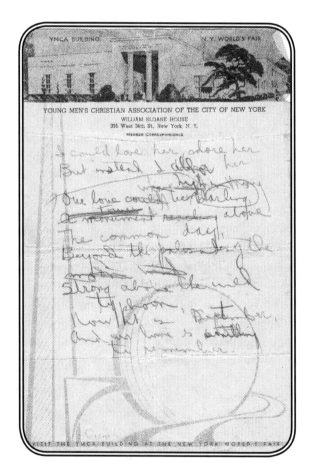

Everett was wrestling with the very deep-seated dichotomy of women as madonnas or whores. Gretchen's revelation about having had a venereal disease was beginning to eat at him. Debasing her was a way of gaining control. Gretchen was a very competent, older woman who was more free-spirited and experienced in the world than my father was. Living up to the expectations of such a woman may have become frightening for him. In marrying her, he may have bitten off more than he could chew.

He had just been rejected by the army as not good enough physically and was most likely living off Gretchen's earnings from the Drake. He could not have been feeling good about himself as a man in an era when "real" men were going off to war and were supposed to be their families' breadwinners. His rejection by the army may have stirred up emotions about rejection by his mother. The poems he wrote late in his college career come to the forefront—love was a dangerous emotion. The fascination with Gretchen was clearly over. From the documents available to me, I have little else to account for this change. He did not take up with other women.

Gretchen worked at the Drake until March 5, 1943, when she joined Everett in New York in the apartment he had rented in Jackson Heights, Long Island (now Queens), from which he could easily commute to work on the subway. They had been married a little over a year; during that time, they had spent just one month and occasional days in each other's company. Gretchen was two months pregnant with me at the time. She sensed immediately that my father's affection for her had waned. In a medical interview years later, she dated her suspicions of my father's having cheated on her to March 1943.

The move to New York would have been an extremely stressful and lonely experience for my mother. She was quitting her dream job to join her husband and leaving behind her vast network of friends. She was pregnant; her life of married domesticity had thus begun. She must at least at first have felt her life in New York was very dull compared to her life in Chicago. And she had a husband who had grown distant and who was consumed by his work as he was to be all his life. He was not around much, and their sex life must have suffered. It is no wonder that in such an atmosphere, my mother began to think that my father was having affairs. She was not used to being neglected by men. And my father certainly would not have talked with her about his emotions. As he once wrote to his sister about his childhood, "I knew it was my duty to look happy and not to complain about anything ... As a result, I never said much of anything about my true feelings."

I have no idea what my mother did at that time. I am sure she would have made friends, but I have no knowledge of any specific activities except for one poorly exposed photograph of her working in a garden. Perhaps it was a Victory Garden, planted on private land at the urging of the government to help with food shortages.

I was born on August 17, 1943. It was not a wonderful experience for my mother. In an effort to reduce infant mortality rates, the medical community tried to limit outside contact with the mother and baby—no father by the bedside coaching his wife in Lamaze techniques. My mother spoke of being left alone, strapped down to the bed, and calling out in pain.

The standard method to reduce pain at the time involved drugging the mother by giving a combination of a painkiller and scopolamine derived from the poisonous belladonna plant to induce forgetfulness of any pain experienced. Nurses reported, however, that mothers did shriek in pain and were often restless. Scopolamine can create temporary psychosis.[7]

Shortly after my birth, my mother suffered a major paranoid episode obviously building on suspicions she already harbored. I do not know whether scopolamine played a role; there is no current research linking the drug with paranoia. My brother, who worked for major drug firms during his career, believes that it is likely it had some effect on her. Nana had come to be with my mother at that time and referred to my mother's condition as a nervous breakdown.

In the intake report to Independence State Mental Health Institute, where my mother was eventually committed, Nana reported,

> The patient phoned her mother three nights in
> a row at that time to come down at once. When
> the mother arrived she immediately sensed

things were not as they should be. The patient had complained that the room was wired and that they should not talk very loud or else the husband would be able to hear them. She mistrusted her husband and thought he was having an affair with one of her girlfriends. The patient even went to the expense of having a dective [*sic*] follow him. There was no truth what so ever to her suspicions. The mother returned the patient to her home and she snapped out of this difficulty without hospitalization.

There are no extant hospital records from this time, so we do not know if her doctor was concerned about her mental condition. Certainly, her family sought no help for her. No one asked why she held these suspicions or what was behind them; such emotional details were apparently not open to discussion.

Freud argued that psychoses as bizarre as they may be usually have some basis in the real world. In my mother's case, the paranoia she exhibited probably resulted from her sensing that my father no longer loved her. In addition, she had uneasiness about my father's work (hence the reference to the room being wired). This was an uneasiness as mentioned earlier that other people shared about my father's occupation.

Despite all the trials and tribulations, however, my birth was a welcome one. My mother kept a baby book, and there is no evidence that she failed to bond with me. She has a first picture of me; all the statistics regarding my birth such as time, place, weight gain over my first month; and gifts I received. She reported, "Had slight cold at hospital, however, was a fine normal healthy baby."

Long-distance calls were quite expensive, so I suspect my father announced my birth to his parents via a telegram. My father sent a follow-up postcard to his mother saying "Baby's name—Roberta Ann. How do you like it? Both Gretchen and Robbie [my nickname, I hated it] doing swell ... Baby's cute as a bug's ear."

I was baptized in the Catholic Church at St. Joan of Arc in Jackson Heights

on September 19, 1943, with my maternal grandmother and grandfather serving as godparents. Obviously since my grandfather served as my godparent, the breach that occurred with my mother upon her marriage had somehow been healed. But according to my father, I was listed in the registry as a "bastard" as he and my mother had not been married in the church. That haunted my mother later in life.

While the breach with my maternal grandparents was apparently healed, there was an obvious breach between my parents. My birth precipitated serious tensions about religion. My grandmother Pearl wrote to her daughter Christine after a visit by Everett in February to see his parents in Baldwin.

He is much worried. He and Gretchen have been having serious differences over the Catholic angle (as we feared). He consented to having a priest baptize the baby, but there are other steps that he feels impossible. She wants him to have a priest "bless" their marriage which would mean for him to sign promises to have any children raised in the Catholic church *and school.* The latter is his greatest objection tho' [*sic*] all is against his wishes. He doesn't know what the outcome will be. He wants Robbie to have a natural "rounded out" bringing up and is quite unhappy over it all as that was his objection before marriage. He doesn't altogether blame Gretchen as it is the way she was brought up. There seems to be more disappointments in life than anything else ... He said Gretchen tho' [*sic*] lots of me and said "if they got a divorce" she wanted to keep in touch with me, which was unique. I am fond of her and hope they will adjust it. You see the way they look at it according to her church they are not really married which I told him was an insult all around. She changed her ideas since the baby was born. Well, maybe by the time she is tied up again to all the domination [by the Catholic Church] she will get tired of it all again. Of course we won't discuss it with anyone now, at least. Wish he had not married yet.

Chapter 6

Wartime Separation

Soon after my birth, my father, eager to promote his career and, as was the pattern throughout his life, to escape the emotional tension at home, simply left. He volunteered to go overseas to a job as close to that of a war correspondent as he at his age and experience could possibly expect. He accepted an assignment to go to London to work for the Allied Press Service, part of the Psychological Warfare Division of SHAEF (Supreme Headquarters Allied Expeditionary Force), General Dwight Eisenhower's central command.

So on January 30, 1944, my mother and I went by train to her parents' home in Dubuque. Up to that point, my father's parents in Baldwin had not seen me. My mother had written to her mother-in-law and must have included a picture of me because Pearl reported to Christine that she had taken a picture to show to friends and was somewhat annoyed that at one home, everyone was more interested in playing chess than admiring me.

My father eventually followed my mother; he stopped off in Baldwin at the end of February to see his folks before going to Dubuque. Pearl wrote,

> We just got back a bit ago from seeing Everett off on the bus. We ate a late dinner at Ellen's. Tho't [*sic*] we would feel a little more festive that way than to eat a last dinner at home, before going so far. It is hard to keep from feeling heavy-hearted, but still have to feel he is going into something to use his ability and ambition.

From Dubuque, my father wrote his mother.

> Robbie has grown a lot and is quite a big girl now. She was a little distant with me at first but soon became chummy. She can stand up now for a little while as well as sit up, which makes her feel very, very important. She may [unreadable] the hearts of everybody, and it is going to be a tough job to keep from spoiling her. Gretchen looks 100% and is feeling a lot better.

My father returned to New York and set out for London in March 1944. He was to be gone for two and a half years. By the time he returned, my parents would have been married almost five years but had actually lived together a total of a little over a year.

My father traveled to England as part of a military convoy. The trip was potentially hazardous as German submarines were on the lookout to sink Allied vessels. It was a rough passage, and most of his fellow passengers got seasick and could not enjoy the food, which he found delicious.

Meanwhile back in the states, the new grandparents exchanged Christmas cards

My father is on the right.

and at some point in the new year, my grandmother Pearl went to Dubuque to visit me. She did speak her mind in a letter to Gretchen, however, as she later informed Christine.

> Yes, it seems as if people are often spoiled by too much "Religion" but not by real Christianity and all the forms and ceremonies and Pharisaical heaviness that cover up true inner rightness is a hindrance rather than a help. I said something of that in my letter to Gretchen and told her that faith in Jesus Christ was the center of both Catholic and Protestant beliefs. He said "The kingdom of Heaven is within you" and all these forms caused divisions. Felt like there should be a little more understanding about it. Seems to be "Religion vs. Christianity." I suppose Mary's [the Virgin Mary's] nice ways can affect her religious bias but there is something peculiarly trying to have people sound and act so pious

and be unfair. Of course Gretchen <u>doesn't</u> act pious!!

The line in the sand was slowly being drawn.

My mother led a rather staid life in Dubuque. She lived with her mother and father for several months before finding an apartment. "I worked for a while and then I quit and stayed home being a housewife." I do not know what kind of job she tried; working obviously had no attraction at the time. She would have socialized a great deal with her old girlfriends in Dubuque, who themselves had young children and whose husbands were most likely serving overseas as well. There must have been worry and tension about the progress of the war. In the end, for her as for so many other wives, it was a waiting game.

My mother threw a first birthday party for me she noted in my baby book: "Roberta entertained 7 guests. She received many lovely gifts and beamed from ear to ear and danced when we sang 'Happy Birthday.'" But the tug of the good times she had had in Chicago was still there.

On my second birthday, she took me to a supper club. "Out to dinner at the Sportsman's Club. Robbie throwing kisses at the organ player and helping him play the organ." That is my first childhood memory and one of my fondest. Not until years later did I realize how unusual it was to take me to such a venue.

My mother also took trips to Chicago, where Christine recalled I was so interested in everything that I would dart into stores and behind counters. In the end, my mother put a child's harness on me. I can imagine that I was paraded up and down Michigan Avenue perhaps in my rabbit's fur coat that my father sent me from overseas or in one of the hand-smocked dresses or pinafores Nana made for me.

I quite naturally do not remember what my mother and I did aside from the visit to the Sportsman's Club, but I am sure that I did not lack for attention and praise. I built a healthy self-esteem that I would desperately need later.

In the intake report for the Independence Mental Health Institute, Nana stated that "Gretchen's behavior at that time was fairly normal except that she overemphasized sexual comments and things pertaining to sex in her conversation at that time." At the time, people did not consider sex as proper to talk about publicly, so how frequent and blatantly sexual the comments actually were is hard to gauge. What one could say in Chicago may not have been what was proper to mention in Dubuque. My mother was breaking the social mores.

I have no correspondence between my parents during the two and a half years they were separated, but I am sure they corresponded, and my father did send back photos. But I do know that in London, my father was leading a far more exciting life than my mother was. As for many men of his generation, participation in the war was probably one of the most significant events of his life. In an unpublished novel he wrote years later, he described the Allied Press Service newsroom where he worked. The journalists produced news favorable to the Allied cause as well as news stories such as figures on sheep production that carried clandestine meanings for underground groups in Scandinavia as well as the rest of Europe. The building in which it was housed was right across from the BBC, which itself broadcasted coded messages to resistance groups in Europe twice daily.

The newsroom was a bustling place with blackout curtains covering all the windows although the Nazis had ceased their air attacks on London by the time my father arrived. It was an open room with no separate offices except for the higher-level administrators, who were members of the military.

The writers were civilians as was my father. There was a central news desk where a "slot man" sat at a horseshoe-shaped desk with the American journalists seated on the outer perimeter with their typewriters at the ready. Each American journalist would be handed an assignment to work into a news story. They worked alongside the foreign news desks staffed by refugees from various countries who translated news stories for transmission to their countrymen.

Ultimately, the proofed and approved copy of a news story went by teletype to the Psychological Warfare Division main communication center for wireless transmission abroad. The Allies knew the Nazis monitored these transmissions; hence their usefulness in misleading the Germans about Allied strength and intentions.

In fact, the biggest role that the Allied Press Service played was in the disinformation campaign (codename Fortitude) to mislead the Nazis about when and where the D-Day invasion of Europe would occur. That was a huge effort involving many other activities and agencies. According to my father's novel, the Allied Press Service's task was "to give credence to the imaginary FUSAG (First United States Army Group) attack on the Pas de Calais area by transmitting wireless news reports and messages that would make enemy monitors believe that the invasion there was the main one."

FUSAG did not actually exist, but much effort was exerted in making it seem real including creating dummy aircraft and dummy airfields. It was supposedly stationed at Dover, right across the English Channel from Pas de Calais. Eisenhower put General George Patton, who had a formidable reputation among the German high command, in charge. Patton had been temporarily suspended from regular command for slapping a battle-weary soldier in Sicily.

My father did not live in barracks; he shared an apartment with several other men. While Hitler's forces were no longer flying bombing missions over England, German scientists had developed the V-1, an early cruise missile nicknamed the buzz bomb due to the sound it made before diving. The first attack of V-1s was launched on London one week after D-Day.

My father told me later that he had written a poem for me called "Why Robins Run" in the midst of a buzz-bomb attack. I so wanted to read the poem written especially for me, and I asked about it a number of times. But my father never gave it to me. I was very disappointed. I came across it among his collection of poems after his death. It would have charmed me no end. I don't know why he never looked for it and gave it to me as a child. He apparently did not understand that it meant a lot to me because he talked about it so much. My father was as my brother describes him emotionally dense; he could not easily fathom the emotional effects of his words and actions on those around him. It was to prove a major failing for those close to him.

My father may have had occasional flings while overseas, but that is pure speculation on my part. In the novel he wrote late in life about World War II—a goal he had had from his early days as a writer finally achieved—he imagined the protagonist Jon as the son of a French woman and an American diplomat assigned to posts in Europe. Jon, who had worked as a newspaper reporter and editor in Chicago, enlisted in the air corps as a pilot and had a tour of duty with a B-17 bomber group in England before being transferred to the Allied Press Service. That was quite a conflation of the real and the ideal—the actual work my father performed at the Allied Press Service, his dream of being a pilot, his knowledge of the missions behind enemy lines undertaken by men who had French mothers and who thus spoke French fluently, and his experience later as a diplomat.

Jon's working at the Allied Press Service was actually a cover for a daring undercover mission in France. While working in London, he has a flirtation with a character named Elaine, a British former model and fashion magazine writer who worked in the newsroom where Jon worked. That too was a cover as she participated in Jon's undercover mission later in the novel. He was attracted to her when he first saw her, and he soon pursued her in a very direct manner—asking her to go on a weekend together at their first meeting over tea. She accepted.

In the course of their weekend together, Jon told Elaine that he was married. She was not shocked. Jon explained,

> I married Marian soon after Pearl Harbor was attacked and the United States declared war. We hadn't gone together very long before we were married, but we were affected by the

uncertainty of the future and decided to marry as a way of establishing a lasting relationship, we hoped. Three weeks after we were married I enlisted in the Air Corps, which it was called at that time. If I hadn't enlisted, I would have been drafted and wouldn't have had a free choice to join the Air Corps, which was the branch of service that I wanted. After I left for training we had little chance to spend time together, except for a few weekends before I was transferred overseas. To make a longer story short, we have drifted further and further apart. And that's the way it is. I don't feel married, but I have to admit that I am.

That described almost exactly the scenario of his marriage to my mother, and it is hard to believe it was not a real reflection of his feelings. In the final version of the novel, Elaine resisted Jon's advances, but Jon did bed Brandy, a less-formidable married women and secretary to one of the military men overseeing the Allied Press Service.

In real life, my mother received a letter addressed to him from a young German woman that she placed in her scrapbook with the comment, "poor Fraulein." I imagine it fueled her distrust of him.

In August 1945, one month before the Allied Press Service was closed in London as its work was done, my father was transferred to the Information Control Division Headquarters of the United States Forces European Theater, the American military headquarters involved in occupying Germany. He was stationed in Luxembourg and handled teletype and radio communications with Paris, London, and New York and transmission facilities to Bad Nauheim, Germany, over which an American news file was sent for dissemination to German papers in the U.S. Zone of Occupation. Again, this must have been an exciting time in his life; from my child's point of view, that was confirmed by the fact that he rode a motorcycle!

A CHILDREN'S STORY

W H Y   R O B I N S   R U N
STOP, LOOK, AND LISTEN

Once many, many years ago
Before the times of which we know
There lived a Fairy Queen so gay
Who ruled the land of Happy Play.

All of her subjects you have seen
On Dreamland's sweet and passing screen
Pert pixies clad in elfin blue
With buttons bright as morning dew
Who danced on grasses thru the night
Before the Queen to her delight,

And golden sunbeams in the day
That still a moment could not stay
But danced flitted all about
The Queen's rose throne, in and out.

But the one the Queen loved most of all
Was her little daughter, just so tall
She was the Princess of the land
And on her head she wore a band
Of angel jewels, so bright and rare
They glistened like the morning air.

Her dress of which she was so proud
Was spun soft from a fleecy cloud
And when she toddled out to play
The pixies scattered in her way
Their mantles down upon the ground
To soften the earth should she fall down.

                        ****

And so the realm long, long did stay
Brim full of laughter, light and play
Until one dark, unhappy day
The Princess far away did stray
Into the land of Never-Should-Be

She ran after a butterfly, you see,
Who flittled about so carelessly
With his velvet wings and winking eye
That she lost her way and started to cry.

more

Wartime Separation

WHY ROBINS RUN....2

Back in the kingdom I cannot tell
Of the sorrow and sadness that swiftly fell
Over the Queen and all her subjects as well
When they could not find their Princess fair.

The pixies and sunbeams searched everywhere
In the meadows, forests, down by the brooks
They even looked through the pages of books
The pixies and sunbeams no more would dance
But sat around sadly all in a trance
While the Queen called hopelessly
"My sweet little Princess, come back to me."

❈❈❈❈❈❈❈❈❈❈❈

But in all of the kingdom there was just one
From whom all hope had not yet gone
He was the Queen's messenger, Good Robin his name
Whose duty it was to tell when spring came.

"Fair Queen," cried Good Robin, "be not dismayed"
"I'll find the sweet Princess, where'ere she has strayed."

Off high in the sky Good Robin flew
Above the treetops and puffy clouds, too,
Over the moon he winged on his way
Far into the night until the next day.

At last, far ahead, Good Robin could see
The dark, lonely land of Never-Should-Be.
Down, down Good Robin flew, and there just below
Was the sweet little Princess, asleep in the snow.

Cried Good Robin, "Princess, come, let us go."
She opened her eyes, smiled, and said low,
"Good Robin, up in the sky"
"I'd so like to come...but I cannot fly."

"Then, fair Princess, I'll walk by your side"
And through this strange land I'll be your guide."
And so they went, the Princess fair
With Robin leading with great care
They traveled far for many a day
Until they reached the land of Happy Play.

more

73

WHY ROBINS RUN.....3

From border to border how fast the news spread
The pixies and sunbeams, once filled with dread
Now sparkled with laughter, danced wildly, and said,
"Our Princess, sweet Princess, has come back again,
"Our joy is complete and will never end."
And the Fair Queen, so happy was she
That she cried quite enough for three.

The little Princess told her the story
Of how Good Robin, to his glory,
Had traveled far and there had found
The Princess asleep, and then came down
And led her safely on the ground,
Running ahead to see if all was clear,
Stopping, looking, listening hard to hear
If danger to the Princess could be near.

The Fair Queen at once decreed
That for his brave and glorious deed
All robins should wear upon their throat
A patch of red his courage to denote
And always robins should remain
Just as Good Robin, the very same.

And so that's why to this day
Robins stop, look, then run a little way.

                         ....Ev Reb

Chapter 7

Back in Washington, DC

In December 1945, my father finally returned home. I was over two and a half years old. My mother's entry in my baby book for that Christmas was nothing if not happy.

> Daddy Home (our nicest Xmas gift) Xmas at our little apartment. Stockings hung with care, a Christmas tree (large) and Santa brought Robbie [a whole lot of things]. A trip to Topeka, Kansas [where my father's parents had moved] just before Christmas made it twice as grand.

Pearl gave my mother a blue plastic apron for Christmas, a sure signal that she should play the domestic role as Pearl did.

The position my father secured was with the State Department, Division of International Press and Publications. He worked his way up to being chief of the Air Bulletin Section in 1948 and then chief of the Press Features Section in 1951. He was a man on the make in the best sense of the term. In November 1952, he was named chief of the Middle East Bureau of the United States Information Agency with a government rating of GS-15, the highest civil servants could rise without their appointments being approved by Congress.

Given what went on in his mind before and what happened later, I do not think my father retained much if any love for my mother, but I think he wanted to make a go of the marriage because of me. Divorce was much stigmatized in those days, and no-fault divorce did not exist. Had there been a divorce, my mother most certainly would have had custody of me. In addition, there were initially no great emotional issues; things went relatively smoothly. My father could live with that.

In the postwar world to which he returned, the overwhelming public feeling was that life should return to normal. The men who had won the war were coming home to succeed in peace and to get a piece of the American Dream— good and steady incomes, homes, and families. This of course was nostalgia for a simpler America that never really existed in which the nuclear family was the family unit and the husband went off to work as the breadwinner with the wife staying home to manage the household and kids.

This ideal as depicted in the advertising media and even the textbooks used to teach young kids to read such as the Dick and Jane books[8] was the efficient housewife dressed in a beautifully starched shirtdress and high heels and utilizing the latest consumer devices for the home, which she decorated and kept immaculate. There were no major problems in Dick and Jane's world. Magazine articles encouraged women to leave the workforce, which they had joined to help in the war effort, and devote themselves to being wives and mothers. It was the husband's job to make the money and the wife's to create the best home she could. "The love of a man for his home with its atmosphere of contentment is at least one anchor (and a strong one) calculated to keep him there."[9]

My mother, like the women Betty Friedan later studied in her book *The Feminine Mystique*, took on the housekeeping role. In Dubuque, she had shown no desire to remain in the workforce, but even so much of the housekeeping role must have been fairly boring.

The first place we lived when my father returned to the United States was in an old house in Lanham, Maryland, an unincorporated area about thirteen miles from Washington, DC. We had no close neighbors, and my father took our one car, a canvas-topped convertible. I loved driving around with the top down in fair weather and with the top up during rainstorms, when I could hear the pattering of the drops. I recall having no playmates. I have no memories of my father from that time probably because I saw little of him. The religious issue must have been lying dormant as I recall sensing no tension between my parents or being taken to church. My mother was artistic and worked on a watercolor painting of the house while I made my own attempts at art, the beginning of a lifelong interest and commitment.

Only one memory from this period stands out, and it reveals a certain resourcefulness on my part. My mother had put me in my crib in my upstairs bedroom and told me not to get out while she talked (and to my mind, she talked a lot) with a friend downstairs. I got bored, but I took her admonition literally, so when I needed to have a bowel movement, I stuck my butt over the railing and did it on the floor. Needless to say, she was not pleased, but I do not remember being punished for it.

Soon however, we moved to Washington proper to an apartment complex called McClean Gardens, where I had a lot of kids to play with. Making mud pies (really sand pies) was one of our favorite activities, and my mother had friends among the neighbors. At times, we would all go to drive-in movies, and my father would tickle me with his mustache when he kissed me goodnight. (He had grown one to look older as he was younger than many of his employees.)

I do not remember my mother playing with me much. She did make me lunch every day; my favorite was Campbell's tomato soup with grilled cheese sandwiches, but she did not eat with me. She and I, however, would talk when I went to bed, and she would tell simple stories of her girlhood—the only one I remember involved a cat of hers, which she had taken with her, defecating on a store counter when she was sent to buy something. We thought it funny. When I was worried about the moles on my face, she told me that women in the past considered them beauty marks and used to paste fake ones on. The moles never bothered me after that.

I don't know whether I was too much of a handful for my mother. I do know that for most of my life, I have felt I was "too much" for other people to handle, that I was imposing on them if I spent too much time with them or asked for help. It was an isolating feeling. When I was put in my playpen or crib for extended periods, I would get bored. I remember eating some glass Christmas tree ornament as my playpen was near the tree. Another time while in my crib, I got hold of a pair of scissors and cuts chunks of my hair, which I carefully wrapped in torn pieces of paper from a coloring book. We went to a baseball game, and I loved jumping up and down and cheering until it was clear that my mother had forgotten to put on my underpants, so I had to sit still for the rest of the game.

There were family get-togethers with relatives from both sides, and everyone seemingly got along well together at the time.

Picture of a family outing taken by Nana.

My two grandmothers and me.

The one incident of tension between my parents that I remember came one evening when we were out driving. My mother saw a supper club or nightclub she wanted us to stop at. Reluctantly, my father agreed, but all my parents did was sit silently across from each other at a small table with me on the sidelines. They obviously were at loggerheads, and my father was literally tightlipped. After my mother had one drink, we left. No dancing. I do not know if my father saw that as a waste of money or if he regarded such good times as inappropriate and frivolous at the time.

The year 1947 was the beginning of an extremely stressful time for my mother. Being a housewife in and of itself was hardly without great strain given the prevalent ideal, and more stresses were added to that. Like so many young mothers at the time, my mother became pregnant. I remember her glowing with pleasure when she talked about it with neighbors. My brother, Richard Reb, was born on October 30 that year, a baby boomer. He was one of a record number of babies being born after World War II. As restraints and sedation were used well into the 1950s, it is highly likely that my mother again experienced a birth similar to what she had experienced with mine.[10]

Mom and Ricky

One month to the day Ricky was born, my grandfather, Joseph Richard, died of lung cancer. He had apparently developed cancer as a result of shoveling coal into the furnaces at the Catholic girls' school where he continued to work. My father and mother took me with them to visit him at the Mayo Clinic in Minnesota.

That is my only memory of him. He was very kind and gentle with me, and the last I saw of him was when I had to leave because he needed to get what looked to me like an enormous shot. The doctors opened up his chest but sewed him right back up. There was nothing they could do.

Me, Mom, and my grandparents at the Mayo Clinic

Nana later reported that at that time, my mother began to get suspicious of my father again. "She also became confused and mixed up at times. Her housework started slipping and the husband did have to step in and help her when he returned home in the evening." In other words, she was not living up to her designated role. Again, no psychiatric or other medical help was provided. No one asked why this was happening. The onus was on her to get herself together.

There was, however, no mention of any of this in my parents' letters. In writing to his mother, my father talked proudly of Ricky's growth and how active he was. "Like Robbie, he doesn't seem to require much sleep." At that time, I was having coughing spells that turned out to be allergic reactions. When tested, I was found to be allergic to just about everything including smoke, dust, and feathers. I went to preschool, but my mother frequently had to come get me and take me to the doctor for a penicillin shot as I would run low-grade fevers.

The allergies were due to infected tonsils. At the time, doctors did not believe that kids should have their tonsils out until they were five. So when I turned five, I was taken to the Walter Reed Medical Center for the operation. It was a horrible experience as ether was used as the anesthetic. After the operation, I hemorrhaged and had to have large cotton rolls stuck up my nose. I was alone most of the time as visits even by parents were strictly regulated.

The one-bedroom apartment we lived in was too small, and life for my parents, especially my mother, became more circumscribed. My father wrote in April 1948 that going out with some friends "has been ... about our only recreation. With the kids, the weather, etc. we have stayed very, very close to home ... Gretchen has been pretty tired, especially since the boy is so heavy and big, but is bearing up under the strain."

Chapter 8

The Move to Hyattsville, Maryland

By January 1949, my parents had purchased a small two-bedroom, one-bath home in one of the new suburban developments that sprang up after World War II. Unlike the more well-known Levittown developments, these homes were brick and had basements as well as fireplaces and unfinished second floors.

Twelve homes lined our street, which ended at a dirt road under which a natural creek flowed through a viaduct. Our neighbors were an interesting mix of professional, white-collar families including schoolteachers and a minister as well as blue-collar families whose husbands worked in construction. But as in

Levittown, there were only white residents. In one of the neighboring houses, the husband was Jewish, and the neighbors just ignored him, his wife, and their baby. I would sometimes go next door and be with her and the baby; she seemed so lonely and glad for my visit.

In *The Feminine Mystique*, Betty Friedan referred to the suburbs as "burying people alive." I cannot recall what my mother did during the day. We apparently had a maid at least once a week. My mother no longer painted. There were no stores nearby, and we had only one car. My father occasionally shared rides with a fellow worker each taking turns driving. "Helps the wifes [*sic*] out to have the car once in awhile [*sic*]."

I do not remember my mother having any close friends in Hyattsville except a next-door neighbor. There was not much socializing among the neighborhood women. Every time I visited a particular girlfriend's immaculate house, her mother would be sitting in tight Capri pants and a form-fitting blouse by the window waiting for her husband and tweezing her almost razor-thin eyebrows. She obviously had read all the advice about pleasing your husband.

Otherwise, my parents threw themselves into making their American Dream nest. My mother reported extensively to her in-laws on her progress.

> We painted our cream bedroom furniture white and mother [Nana] made me a beautiful spread out of that green nylon parachute that Everett brought home [from the war] ... My white ruffled curtains (that I used in living room before) in there and our wallpaper is a light

86

pink satin strip. I made a ruffled affair around the dressing table too out of an extra curtain and lined it with rose, however, will exchange that for a green and white flowered chintz later on. The room now looks a little too feminine and must be a bit too much for Ev. Robbie's room is darling. We got a white background paper which has nursery children scattered throughout. Then we bought an old walnut dresser with marble top and painted that up white with trimming in pink. We also painted two bookcases for her room and lined them in pink too. Painted the table and chairs white with pink border and that cedar chest (we had gotten 2nd hand) painted white makes a nice addition to her room too. I painted a bushel basket pink for their toys too ... I'm really proud of her room and it looks so cozy. We are still working on the living room. We got a new Simons-hide-a-bed (which by the way was worth the change as it's so comfortable). We are sure proud of our house and every bit we do makes it that much more interesting and exciting. We bought 2nd hand end-tables and coffee table and plastic covers for the sofa and chair (barrel). The other chair is of plastic material which resembles leather and is washable so we don't have to tip toe through the living room for fear of ruining things. It's considerably kid-proof this way too. For the kitchen we painted backless stools white (they were old chairs with backs) and I made oil cloth covers for them to match our kitchen table cover. Our kitchen table was unpainted and we also painted that. So you see we have done lots of painting. I usually would start things off with a first coat then Ev would finish up with the second.

Besides decorating, Gretchen had considerable concerns about and responsibilities for our family's health. She reported to her in-laws that I had gained weight since moving to Hyattsville. "She's fine and is roughing it and doing things (without bad results) that were unheard of last year at this time. We, as a result, are a much happier and healthier family, all around and are sure glad we had the operation [tonsillectomy] performed."

My mother gave me sunlamp treatments and tried to give me cod liver oil and enormous vitamin pills I had a hard time swallowing. It was a big occasion when I did. She fed my brother and me a glass of milk with a raw egg in the morning, which I can only presume was touted as healthful at the time. In addition, my feet toed in, so I had to wear ugly corrective shoes, which involved more doctor's visits. My mother told me of a relative who had the same problem and that they had to break the bones in his legs and reset them. Not a cheery thought.

The demands on my mother continued to increase. My father found out he was allergic to penicillin.

I had this virus I was trying to get rid of, so I tried penicillin nose-drops as one way. Just the drops—not a shot—was enough. I broke out with hives, my eyes were nearly swollen shut. I went to a doctor and he gave me a[n] adrenaline injection, which helped some. Great red welts appeared all over me, and turned successively white and blue. Meanwhile, they itched. I also had the virus (or flu) with a temperature. That didn't help! I was away from work for a week and one-half.

Gretchen really had her hands full. Robbie was ill home from school, and Ricky wasn't well, either. She also had the virus, so it was a really bad time for her. But she did a fine "nursing" job, and we are all back in the harness. Robbie and Ricky have tendencies toward bronchitis and such, and Gretchen has to be specially careful.

My mother found it hard to keep up appearances as an ideal housewife. She told her in-laws about a visit of wartime friends of Everett's while she was alone at home.

It was a nice surprise but I was very embarrassed as the house was some what [sic] upset and I had an armful of diapers since I was in the basement taking down the washing. [Only cloth diapers in those days, no Pampers. Clothes were lined dried so it must have rained that day and the diapers were hung indoors.] Such is the life of a mother, however, and they took it all in grand spirit.

Our world, however, was not confined entirely to the home. My parents had the thrill of attending the inaugural gala in 1948 when Harry Truman was reelected "and saw all the celebrities perform." As a family, we visited the National Gallery of Art. I, a budding artist, was apparently much impressed. According to my father, I was "something of an artist in temperament and also ability. She draws pictures remarkably well for a six-year-old. Ricky was more interested in the Gallery Guards, with whom he made a great hit."

We went on picnics with friends of my father's, went to the Washington Monument to lie on the grass and watch the fireworks on July 4th, and visited Grandma Pearl, Grandpa Louis, and Aunt Christine in Chicago, managing to give them the flu in the process. We also in the summer would drive to a private beach on Chesapeake Bay and swim or more accurately bob up and down with the waves. My mother was an enthusiastic swimmer; she swam throughout her life from her days at her grandfather's fishing camp to almost the end of her life.

My mother also was in charge of social events from preparing a small, family birthday party for my father to entertaining his office staff at our home. But as my father admitted,

> Most of our social life has been confined to television. We saw the opening of the Metropolitan Opera season ... There's a good movie on every Saturday night. The last one we saw was "Major Barbara," by G. B. Shaw, quite good. Then, of course, there's always

Milton Berle [a famous comedian at the time]
to brighten our lives.

I sensed that my mother projected a lot of herself onto
me. The cod liver oil and sunlamp treatments mentioned
previously were to make sure I had enough vitamin D for
the adequate absorption of calcium, something in which my
mother had been deficient as a child. She had me take tap
and ballet lessons, which was something she had taken as a
teenager and loved. I did not. I was the youngest in the dance
class, and my only nice memory was getting a big peppermint
candy cane from the teacher at Christmas.

My mother admired the child movie star Shirley Temple
and would use an old-fashioned curling iron she heated on the
stove to curl my hair into ringlets like Temple's when I was
going to a party or having a family portrait. I can still smell
the burnt hair. I did not want to be Shirley Temple.

Despite what seems so normal on the surface, Ricky
and I were basically out of control by the time we moved to
Hyattsville. My father's letters sugar coat the situation. In
January, he wrote to his folks,

> Ricky is growing by leaps and so is Robbie ... He
> is a little rascal, always getting into mischief,
> turning on the gas stove, pulling books out of
> the bookcase, eating whatever he can get hold
> of, etc. We keep him in his playpen (for his
> protection as well as ours) until his protests get
> too loud. We really have a couple of whoppers.

Gretchen has been kept plenty busy at home—
don't know [how] she stands the pace. You have
to wrestle Ricky to get his clothes on, and, he
likes to stand on the table to eat instead of sitting
down. Robbie makes plenty of demands, too.
She still thinks mama should be her personal
maid.

Then in June 1949, Everett wrote,

He [Ricky] is a literal live-wire from morn til
night, into drawers, shelves, everything. One
just can't keep up with him. Robbie also gets very
active, and the two together make us somewhat
apprehensive of life and limb when they are
going full-blast ... We have been busy housecleaning, cleaning walls, floors, windows, etc.
The crayon marks on the walls are somewhat
difficult to remove, especially on wallpaper.
Ricky slips a crayon in his little fist and makes
swipes at the walls as he moves through. Since
Robbie likes to color, it is somewhat difficult to
keep crayons from him."

Gretchen added in her own letter to her in-laws that Ricky
was so active that she was "in a constant state as to what will
come next. We now pile the kitchen stools on top of the table
and eliminate all climbing articles (as much as possible) all
through the house. Well I guess he will be over this difficult
age sooner than the slower child [Ricky was ahead of things

for his age] at least I am trying to get some consolation from that thought."

Religion did not seem to be an issue; we never went to church, but I was aware of considerable tension between my parents over other matters. One was Ricky's hair. In a letter to her in-laws, my mother stated, "Ricky is a wonder child and gets cutier [*sic*] and sweeter every day. His hair grows longer and curlier and Ev and I still ain't doing a thing about it." That made it sound as if my parents had been in agreement, but they were not. My mother, who had naturally curly hair, felt that once Ricky's hair was cut, it would not grow back curly, and she wanted to put off that day as long as possible.

In his descriptions of my brother, my father always emphasized masculine qualities. He referred to Ricky as "strong as they make them." In January 1950, he told his folks,

> Ricky is as active as ever, and growing too. He is badly in need of a haircut, and looks somewhat like a girl. The looks are deceiving, however, he is very much boy. There's not a thing in the house that can be put beyond his little fingers. He also has a penchant for breaking dishes. But he is cute with it all.

According to a letter from my father to his mother in May 1949, Ricky had a haircut at that time, almost a year and a half after his birth. It must have been allowed to grow long again as he mentioned the need for a haircut again in a January 1950 letter.

My parents had conflicts about other things I did not know about, but I vividly remember their loud arguing in front of me. I went into the hallway and deliberately started to cry because I knew they would stop arguing and come to comfort me, which they did.

I dealt with the situation inside the house by focusing on my life outside the house. I loved school. In September 1949, I started first grade at Riverdale Elementary. My father commented, "Robbie seems to be doing very well at school, although we don't get too much from her on the subject." Doing well in school was especially important to my self-esteem all my life.

Back then, childhood play was far less structured and supervised than it is today. I was much of a tomboy and could take the rough-and-tumble. A small wood was near the house; rumor had it that an elderly woman owned it and refused to sell it to developers. We kids roamed freely there out of sight of the adult world! I considered the boy next door, Jimmy, as my boyfriend and pal. We would find a spot in the creek at the bottom of the hill to dam up and soak in. He used a stick to scrape the water for water moccasins, and once, he got one wrapped around a stick, which he shook at me with the cotton mouth of the snake clearly visible. I do not remember

94

being especially afraid. He then flung it into the bushes. I do not think we were aware that those snakes were deadly poisonous.

He would also chop a tree half down, climb it, and swing it back and forth until it fell. One day, he and I accidentally set the woods on fire with matches. I ran and got my mom and a door-to-door salesman she had been talking to, and they put it out quickly.

My father was enormously proud of his work; it was a source of self-esteem. The Air Bulletins his office produced consisted of positive, interesting news stories about a variety of topics. These news stories were published at information outposts and distributed to the press in Greece, Egypt, India, Brazil, Sweden, Denmark, Hong Kong, Korea, and elsewhere. Also, being used by radio stations in many countries—most recently in Iceland.

We get reports of wide usage from many points, which is gratifying, make the work seem worthwhile. We also got "praise" from American organizations about which we write and Margaret Truman [daughter of President Harry Truman] sent a personal note of thanks in [*sic*, concerning] a story we wrote about her concert tour. Said she was going to put in the story in her scrapbook. By the way we received a "fan letter" from a librarian at the Univ. of Pittsburgh. She was hard of hearing, and read about a hearing aid device in the Bulletin.

We have to very careful with our medical news, especially new drugs. People abroad read the stories and want some usually urgently—from the American Embassy in their country. In Czechoslovakia one of the major medical publications prints Air Bulletin stories along with those from "other" major medical journals.

Chapter 9

The Beginning of the End of the Marriage

Any semblance of the serene American Dream ended in 1950. That was the year I turned seven, the Cold War was heating up, and even more stressors were besetting my mother. The Korean War began when North Korea, which Russia had occupied after World War II, invaded South Korea, which the United States had occupied. It pitted North Korea, China, and Russia against the American-led United Nations forces.

The same year, Senator Joseph McCarthy of Wisconsin released a statement that he had lists of State Department employees who were Communists. His accusations eventually grew into televised hearings, more like witch hunts, that my father watched avidly. At some point, my father himself was accused of being a Communist sympathizer by a disgruntled former employee he had fired. The charge was apparently that he thought it might be a good idea to get a subscription to *Pravda*, the official Russian Communist Party newspaper, to see what the other side was saying. He had to appear before an internal State Department tribunal and was cleared.

Having had rickets due to a calcium deficiency as a child, my mother's teeth were not in good shape. My father wrote,

> Gretchen has a major teeth project on, and it has sort of interrupted the ordinary course of events. She is going to have all but 6 lower teeth extracted. A full upper plate and a bridge below. Last Friday she had the second of three impacted wisdom teeth out, and it turned out to be a major operation. She was in the dentist chair for well over an hour. The tooth had a lip on it jutting into the bone. The dentist had to chisel the tooth in two, take out one half and then the other. She had two other teeth out at the same time, and the whole business was understandably tough on her. I took off from work on Friday, Monday and Tuesday to take care of the kids. She still is awfully shaky because of her ordeal, and it's going to take quite awhile [sic] before everything is over with. She still has another impacted tooth, three teeth on the side and about 12 teeth in front to come out, not to mention the gold-filling of the six anchor teeth to remain. The dentist has been extracting the teeth each Friday, but after the last encounter I doubt if things can progress that fast in the future.

This is the last sympathetic reference to my mother in my father's correspondence. The removal of the teeth was not only physically grueling on my mother; it was an operation that changed part of her body. For someone who wanted to look good, that must have been particularly frightening. She may have thought it would make her less desirable to my father. It affected her judgment I believe, because she told me it had been my fault that she had used up her calcium having me. I thought that strange and mean. She of course would have been given heavy doses of painkillers at the dentist's that may have helped alter her mental state.

In February 1950, my mother reached a breaking point, and "apparently" (my father's qualification) deliberately drove the family automobile into a telephone pole. She did not seem to need any medical treatment. My mother was not a very good driver; I had been with her when she had an accident with another car. She was not quoted in any correspondence as telling people she was trying to commit suicide. So I do not know why my father and Nana regarded this as a suicide attempt, particularly as they did not act to get her psychiatric help.

Chapter 10

Back to Dubuque

In March 1950, my mother decided to visit her mother in Dubuque and have the remainder of the dental work done there. She took my brother and me with her. But I think she had an ulterior motive to go at that time.

In the very same month, she obtained a copy of my baptismal certificate as a necessary prelude to my receiving my first Holy Communion in May. I went to the parochial school my mother had attended in Dubuque. Religion was becoming an issue, and I was at the center of it. She apparently wanted me to have the experiences she had had and did not feel obliged to honor the agreement she and my father had made before their marriage.

Me in 1950 looking like a deer caught in headlights

The parochial school was very dark, and I was rather frightened of the nuns in their black habits and the click-click of their hard-soled shoes on the tile floor as they patrolled the halls.

I vaguely remember catechism classes to prepare me for my first Communion. I learned the Catholic version of the Lord's Prayer, the Nicene Creed, and the Hail Mary, and I learned how to cross myself, all of which I remember to this day. I enjoyed wearing a white dress and veil and processing into the church to become a

bride of Christ. I took it all very seriously. I even wondered if it was okay to bite the communion wafer, which stuck to the roof of my mouth, as it was the body of Christ. In the end, I just sucked on it.

Nana owned an apartment building that had been a former soda pop factory; it had been converted into several small apartments with oddly arranged rooms. The one we stayed in had only one bedroom, which my mother took. Ricky and I slept on roll-away beds brought out at night and set up in one of the two contiguous parlors. There was no hot water or regular bathroom with a tub and shower. The toilet was in a small closet area next to the kitchen sink, probably a former pantry. Ricky and I bathed in a big washtub with water that had been heated on the stove—no privacy. I played with neighborhood kids but knew none of them well enough to consider them my friends.

Some years later, Nana told my brother that our mother was under a lot of stress from the dental work and the pain it entailed, but that was not surprising. On top of that, she had a sore shoulder due to a piece of bone that had broken loose from the joint capsule. She received some sort of physical therapy for it and quite conceivably more painkillers. Again, the painkillers she took for her teeth extractions and shoulder could have contributed to her psychological issues.

After my mother, Ricky, and I went to Dubuque, my father's mother came to visit him. I do not know if he had asked her to come or if she had taken the initiative herself. Knowing her, she had probably taken the initiative. The line in the sand was drawn. She heard from my father about his experience of my mother's behavior toward him, and that led to my father's writing to Nana detailing these behaviors.

I do not have a copy of the letter and can only reconstruct the issues that caused tensions from letters and information provided by my father and grandmother at my mother's admission to the mental institution. As is often the case in marriages, money played a role, but I think a very small one in this instance. My mother never apparently directly mentioned it. But my father worried about money all his life; that worry seemed to underlie a feeling of guilt perhaps that he was not living up to his end of the American Dream. He wrote about taking only $20 a month for expenses.

> Gretchen didn't seem to have too much either, nor the kids. I make about $8,000 a year [about $80,000 in today's money] and yet we never had enough, and the *impression* [my italics] was definitely given that I didn't provide properly for my family. One wonders why people with less money had more. Then one realizes that in a family where love does not exist, nothing works.

The latter is of course an irrational explanation as far as not having enough money is concerned and surprises me to this day. It sounds like a reflection of his own family's situation where money was always tight and love between his parents did not exist.

From my experiences later in life, I know my mother was not a big spender and that my father was not a good money manager; he was penny wise and pound foolish. He told me once that he had not taken me and my brother to see the dentist when we were kids because the dentist would have told him we needed braces, which were expensive. He would agonize over filling out income tax forms looking for every deduction he could muster including the pencil he used in making calculations. Yet when he borrowed money from his government pension to purchase a small-town newspaper, following in the footsteps of his hero William Allen White, he tried to restore the funds several days after the deadline for doing so had passed and as a consequence lost his right to receive a pension.

He suddenly bought two motels in New Mexico, sold his interest in the newspaper in New York for a song, and loaded up a van with what possessions would fit to return to New Mexico all within a week and a half. He didn't bother selling the house in New York first; he left it filled with furniture and took a loss on the sale of that too.

Another issue raised in regard to my mother was housekeeping. As mentioned earlier, Nana reported that shortly after my brother was born, Gretchen's "housework started slipping and the husband did have to step in and help her when he returned home in evening." I do not know if Nana knew that by having seen it firsthand or had learned it from my mother or father.

In a letter to his mother, Everett wrote, "I cannot tell you how hard I struggled to make things work, including doing many of the household chores and taking care of the children." Apparently, my mother was not living up to her role in achieving the American Dream. Running an efficient and beautiful home while raising children was her responsibility, and in their eyes, she was not meeting it, and that was a sign of trouble. It probably was but not in the sense of lax attention to household chores; it was perhaps because neither my mother nor my father seemed to know how to properly discipline and handle us kids and the chaos we created. It was his failure to set proper limits as well as hers.

My father certainly thought of housework and raising children as woman's work. Years later when he had remarried, he expected my stepmother to do the same, and when my stepmother went off in the summers to spend weeks visiting her folks, I was expected to do the cooking and cleaning as well as taking on a summer job. He and my brother made no offers of help with the chores.

What most disturbed my father and Nana, however, involved the same issues as after my birth—religion, sex, and my father's work in psychological warfare. In response to my father's letter detailing what was happening, Nana said,

> Well, Gretchen took the children for a walk so I'll at least start an answer to you. Yes dear I was shocked to hear G was acting like that. I have told her so many times you should come first and then the children. She seems to have a complex about the children and Religion ... Now Evie it's immaterial to me if they go to a Catholic school, but Robby will go there till we go [back] to W. [Washington, DC] It [the Catholic school] was so much closer and G wanted it. And she [Robby] will make her communion and then it will be easier ... I sure feel sorry for you Dear.

My take on this is that my mother wanted me to be a reflection of her and enjoy what she had enjoyed including the camaraderie fostered in a Catholic girls' school and the pleasure she found in church rituals. That she had married someone who did not support that way of raising me should have come as no surprise to her particularly as they had discussed it before their marriage. But my mother paid that no mind. Years later, she told me, "Your father would have made such a good Catholic." But that was certainly never in the cards.

In the intake report to the mental institution, Nana explained that Everett was not Catholic and that Gretchen "worries some about this fact but he is very tolerant and allows her to bring up the children in that church." It is obvious Nana was not aware of the depth of my father's feelings on the issue of my attending parochial school. Everett wrote to his mother,

> There are a good many reasons why I did not give my consent [to my attending Catholic school in Maryland], and I think that they pretty well explain the nature of the whole problem. For one thing, the separation of church and school for the children was agreed upon at the very beginning and was a basis for going through with the marriage. For another thing, I feel just as sincerely and firmly in my views on the subject as Gretchen hers. I felt that consenting to bring them up in the Catholic Church was a major concession in the first place, and that public schooling was only fair. But more importantly, it would give the children a more balanced outlook on life. It would otherwise become unbearable as the years went by to see them take attitudes that were entirely foreign to my own, and to what I believe is right.

In making his report to the Independence Mental Health Institute, my father listed fears and occasional depressions as two of Gretchen's symptoms. But because she had not seen a psychiatrist up to that point, these "depressions" cannot be considered clinical. The specific fears mentioned in the letters related to whether I would be going to Catholic school and, as after my birth, her concern that my father was unfaithful and had used propaganda. From comments in Nana's intake report, my mother had been concerned about "wires" and "somebody keeping tab[s] on her." That was probably related to her fears of my father's occupation. He was obviously having difficulty coping with the worries my mother expressed. He apparently could not handle the emotional tension, and his way of coping was to give in, which in turn caused resentment on his part.

My mother's "fears" seemed unending to him.

> This is extremely important to understanding the situation, my consenting to send the children to Catholic School would result in only a "temporary peace." For it is the very nature of Gretchen's mental illness that her mind would then seize upon another worry that would over-burden her. In other words, the next thing might be that since I'm non-Catholic, I must become Catholic to give her peace of mind. After that, there would be still another problem.

> There is no way to express the tension that was falsely created. Even when things were going smoothly on the surface, no one could enjoy the better times because they knew it wouldn't last and didn't know when and how it would end.

Usually when things were going smoothly, it was a sign that things were going to pop ... It is so easy to lose sight of the fundamental basis of her problem. She has a wonderful facility for appearing to be a warm-hearted, gentle, generous person, of doing only what is best for her children and her husband. She definitely wants people to think such is the case, and acts sufficiently well to give most that impression. I, for one, was definitely fooled.

I do not think my mother was trying to fool anyone. As I mentioned earlier, she came from a background in which getting mad at or having conflicts with someone was part and parcel of life while my father came from a home that had been made tense by his mother. Conflict was to be avoided. His view that Gretchen was faking being nice has for me the overtones of the poems he wrote about not being allowed access to the inner life of a woman he desired and the fear of holding the "empty shell" of a lover who just laughed at him.

My mother does not appear to have been passive-aggressive; my father reported that she "did not have a bad temper." He certainly felt, however, that he was made

to walk a narrow path, the course of which is set by her whims, her frustrations and fears, and changed without a moment notice ... What if despite all your efforts you stray from that narrow path, and are literally considered worse than a common criminal and must do penance for wrong acts which exist only in her imagination.

We know from my mother's comments in her scrapbooks that she could be dismissive of men who did not behave as she thought they should. Perhaps there was an element of that here. There also could have been resentment on her part for his lack of fulfilling her sexual desires (as discussed later). Maybe she provoked him in an effort to get his attention.

My father had a peculiar blindness about people. He wanted to do what he wanted to do and did not foresee consequences. Particularly, he did not see how his actions affected the feelings of those around him. When he was taking on an overseas assignment for the State Department in Beirut, Lebanon, in the late 1950s, he never told my brother and me that we were going with him. He decided at the last minute to remarry and chose a woman my brother and I had met only once or twice before their wedding, which took place one day before we sailed for Beirut.

He had chosen someone who was rather introverted and passive and who was really not equipped to be a mother although she tried. She was certainly not one to challenge his authority. When we got to Beirut, our stepmother's father died, and she wanted to return for his funeral as she had been particularly close to him. My father would not allow that as it would have been too expensive; they sent flowers instead. My stepmother never seemed quite the same after that episode, and she too ultimately had psychological problems.

Later, when he was putting together the money to buy the newspaper in New York, he raided my savings account; I had saved money from my various jobs to buy clothes for college. I learned about it only when I went to take the money out. When I confronted him about that, he brushed it aside. My father's own behavior most likely played a role in my mother's developing mental illness.

My father also mentions "fancies" as another of my mother's symptoms. Fancies were whims as he mentioned in the quote above, and I am sure my mother was given to whims. Letting my brother's hair grow had been one. Fussing over the color of a chair for the living room was another. Her burning candles in wine bottles so the wax would drip all over them and give them, as she told me, a bohemian look was a whim. I think my mother enjoyed her whims; they enriched life for her, but my father did not understand that. I think he wanted a more predictable home life.

My father got more than he bargained for in his wife and was overwhelmed. She needed somehow to be brought under control as he could not deal with it. Rather than admit this to himself, he found it easier to define her as mentally ill. That was an easy label, and as her concerns and desires were not met, it became a self-fulfilling prophecy. The idea of consulting a marriage counselor did not occur to him. It would have involved probing his emotions, something he wanted to avoid.

The major problem, however, centered on my mother's sexual desires; their being unfulfilled led to her paranoia about my father's sex life. My father referred to them in the intake report as "extreme suspicions." One piece of information that I know for sure was in the letter my father sent to Nana was that my mother was asking for sexual intercourse four times a night, and according to my father, her desire was increasing. I suspect this was a gross exaggeration and doubt whether this was a nightly occurrence. Having masturbated, she knew what an orgasm felt like; my suspicion is that when making love with my father, my mother was not climaxing and consequently was feeling frustrated and wanted release.

It may also be that having sex with him was her way of testing whether he loved her. He did not love her, and therefore, having sex was probably not something he sought. He came from a very sexually repressed family, and that would have made her sexual demands seem overwhelming. In his report to the mental institution, he characterized my mother's sexual orientation as "mixed." Had she told him about her mutual masturbation with girls, or had she wanted to try sexual positions other than the missionary one?

That was an era when females' sexual desire was not much understood or considered even a proper topic for discussion or research even in medical schools. It was swept under the rug until 1953, when Kinsey published *Sexual Behavior in the Human Female.* Kinsey's findings challenged the entrenched thinking on female sexuality and the primacy of patriarchy, i.e., that the female was the passive partner and the satisfaction of the male was the main goal of intercourse.

And it was not until 1966 that William Masters and Virginia Johnson published *Human Sexual Response,* which for the first time documented the complexities of the female sexual response and the fact that unlike men, women were capable of multiple orgasms in a very short time. Kinsey and Masters and Johnson were concerned that male sexual inadequacy in bringing their partners to orgasm would damage the relationship in the "marital unit."[11] Kinsey's data showed that "Even in her marital coitus the average female fails to achieve orgasm in a fair proportion of her contacts ... but in 95 per cent or more of all her masturbation, she does reach orgasm."[12]

My mother was posing the same challenge to established mores as the researchers later did. She was ahead of her time in her frankness. In 1950, she told her mother that my father was not satisfying her sexually and that she "had to resort to self abuse [masturbation]." Nana was horrified at the idea of Gretchen's masturbating. She associated it with insanity, and she told my mother, "she would go insane from such things and she [Gretchen] was really mad. But I tell her the truth."

Beginning with the founding of insane asylums in which doctors could observe patients closely, masturbation was in fact associated with insanity, and patients were admitted to institutions solely for that reason. But by the late nineteenth century, medical professionals had realized that masturbation was a widespread practice and therefore could not be considered a form of insanity; otherwise, most of the population including the doctors would have to have been institutionalized.[13] But such information and change in attitude took a long time to become public knowledge. My grandmother was born in 1889. Old ideas die hard.

When having sex with my father, my mother was obviously not reaching orgasm. In addition, the sex was probably infrequent. When I was an adult, my father told me in another strange communication out of the blue that after the birth of my brother, the doctors said our mother was to have no more children. Since her Catholic beliefs precluded birth control, that made for a difficult situation. I found no reference to doctors saying this in the letters written at the time, but my father certainly felt it was the case and said that one of the critical problems with Gretchen was

> the matter of living together as man and wife. With her illness necessitating no more children on the one hand, and her Catholic beliefs on the other, an impossible situation was induced. Other problems date back much farther, to the very beginning. That was a fundamental lack of faith, understanding, and respect which made me lose them, too.

The revelation about the venereal disease appears to lurk in that statement.

It is within this context that I believe my mother's mental illness needs to be viewed. She developed paranoia about my father's sex life—if he wasn't having sex with her, he must have been having sex with someone else—and that spun off to suspicions about her mother's sex life too. She even told her mother that she, Gretchen, wanted to have sex with her. Had that been for real? Was it possibly a challenge?— If you think I should not masturbate, then have sex with me.

The specifics are scarce, but I know my mother accused my father of sleeping with the African-American maid, and when a wartime friend visited, she apparently "impugned his [Everett's] character" in front of the friend; that may have been anger at his having been sent the letter from the fraulein. She also accused her mother of having sexual relations with Everett and other men.

This was all obviously upsetting and disturbing. She reportedly said to her mother that she "hadn't started on the boys yet." Just what that meant is unclear. My mother used the term *boys* for men—it is how she referred to my father in her comment about him in her scrapbook, but the statement added to the tension about what my mother might do. I emphasize might do because throughout this time, there is no evidence my mother had any extramarital sex, but just the possibility of that was enough to frighten my father and grandmother.

From the information available to me, this constitutes the sum of the issues causing tension and disruption. My mother obviously needed psychiatric help, but she was not psychotic at the time. There is no mention of delusions, only her paranoia about my father's sex life.

It was Nana who finally brought up the issue of seeking psychiatric care. She wrote to my father from Dubuque,

> We have no psyciatrist (don't think this is spelled right) here and I can't leave the children so I'll come there [Washington, DC] and if I were you I'd go to one (phs [*sic*]) and tell him all and then take her. I'll take care of the children

and will cooperate and do all I can and will even help with expenses. We'll have to clear up these suspicions. I believe and trust you Son and lets [*sic*] hope and pray we can get her O.K.

That my father was not sexually satisfying my mother was not of importance to my grandmother. Perhaps she believed that was a woman's lot in life. There is certainly no reference in any of my father's or Nana's letters of the stress my mother was under from her dental work and hurt shoulder. It was as if those could not possibly have played a role in my mother's behavior.

Meanwhile, my father consulted a former classmate from Baker College who had a background in psychology. The man was obviously sympathetic to my father and told him what my father wanted to hear. Without knowing or even meeting my mother, the former classmate gave my father his analysis of Gretchen's situation. My father wrote,

> [The classmate said that] Gretchen's condition was pretty serious and said that she had about a 50 percent change of pulling out of it, he thought. He didn't think she could be a good influence on the children in her condition, but agreed that it would be a tough legal problem to get her judged in court as incompetent to keep them. He thought that her driving into the telephone pole was a sub-conscious expression of her resentment against me ... He thought the best psychiatrists were in Philadelphia and New York, but is going to put me in touch with

a psychiatrist here, who I can talk to. He didn't seem to think there were any good psychiatrists in Chicago. I still feel as strongly as I did that trying to take up together where we left off would be impossible. But the whole thing has to be brought to a head soon, and I'm going to try to reach a definite decision during the coming week on the plan of procedure.

In his letters to his family throughout this period, my father constantly wrote about avoiding the emotional angle and looking at the medical and legal aspects of the problem to come up with the best course of action. He was truly conflicted and was having a hard time facing the situation.

I think it is absolutely necessary, in fact, it is the only way, to think things through carefully before taking any actions. It's so hard to keep emotion from entering into a circumstance like this to a point where it over-rides common sense. The best we can do for the children is to keep sane ourselves. I have to keep reminding myself of this, because I must admit that inclination sometimes tells me to escape, in keeping with the basic law of self-preservation. But obviously the only escape from a problem is to face it—to the best of one's ability.

But he did not face it. No plans were forthcoming from my father. It was Nana who took the initiative. My grandmother had only a sixth-grade education and had grown up in a small community around Fergus Falls, Minnesota, but she was competent and sharp; she knew a thing or two, and she was a doer. If there was a problem, she would find ways to address it.

My father reported to Pearl that Nana had taken the letter he had written while Pearl was there to a doctor

and also told him her own experiences with Gretchen. He seemed to think that electric shock treatments would help her. Then I got a telephone call from Dubuque, and Gretchen said that she had her teeth and was going to take some treatments for her nerves, so maybe that has been settled. Of course, electric shock treatments are pretty drastic and don't always do any good. Their effect is said to be temporary, so they would have to be followed up with regular psychiatric care.

Chapter 11

The Return to Hyattsville and the Lobotomy

In June 1950, it was decided that we all, including Nana, would return to Hyattsville. My father came to pick us up. In her intake interview at Independence State Mental Institute, my mother stated,

> When we were on the road back, he didn't act like he should ... He said that he was only going back for the children's sake. He didn't want me at all. He was rather indifferent. I was very much in love with him, perhaps I acted different because of the disagreement.

Upon arrival, however, my grandmother suffered blood clots in her side and was hospitalized with no definite date set for her release. On June 10, my father reported to his family,

> Although Gretchie, of course, is far from well, she has been doing surprisingly well so far ... She still says some very strange things, but has

been acting pretty normal. She visits her mother every afternoon and night at the hospital, and said the other day that it was the foolish things she had done herself that put her mother in the hospital. The children are getting along quite well. We have been doing a lot of work around the house. I'm starting to put in the basement door, and a very handy neighbor of mine says he will help me get the upstairs in shape. I'm quite anxious to have enough room in the house, so that her mother can stay with us. I feel that, if she is able, she should stay quite a long time ... Don't worry about things here. As of now, they are so much better than they were before that there is no comparison. Because of the kids, I'm going to [do] everything possible to get the situation completely cleared. Gretchen, I know, is trying very hard to combat the tendencies she has.

Almost a month later, on July 7, my father again reported to his family,

We are all getting along about the same here. Mrs. Richard is still in the hospital, and it seems she will be for another week or more. Her blood clots are much better but the clotting substance in her blood is too high and has to be brought down before she can leave the hospital. We have been going up to see her every evening, and Gretchen often goes in the afternoon as well. She seems to be holding up very well, but of course she doesn't feel as much at home as she would in Dubuque.

He reported later still,

> Gretchen is getting along pretty well, but of course she is not completely on top. Her actions are all right, although she drives herself too hard and is under nervous strain, but what she says sometimes indicates clearly that her outlook on life and emotions are not those of a mature person. However, that has been the case for a long time so one can't expect an overnight miracle. We have just been concentrating on getting along all right, and we haven't been doing much until Mrs. Richard gets out of the hospital. She [Gretchen] has been taking chiropractic treatments intermittently, but I doubt very much that they can help to any appreciable degree.

She was taking the chiropractic treatments for her arm; it is unclear whether my father was aware of this or if he thought she was taking the treatments to deal with her emotional condition.

Meanwhile, there were normal activities—going on picnics, my attending a birthday party, and going to a July 4th celebration among them. And my father had his work. "Otherwise we are kept busy around the house and going to the hospital. I have the wall knocked through for the cellar door and hope to get that mostly completed this week end."

From the description in these letters, my mother does not seem to be so seriously disturbed that it interfered with the normal course of life. After all, we kids were in her keeping while my father went off to work. It is thus so hard for me to imagine what happened next. Every time I read the letter describing it, I get upset.

My grandmother came home from the hospital on a Thursday, and within twenty-four hours, my mother was taken to see "a very highly regarded specialist, Dr. Walter Freeman, who made no bones about Gretchen's condition after one interview."

Freeman routinely took head-and-shoulders pictures of his patients, which he used in publications as evidence of their conditions before and after surgery. In almost all the published photographs, the before pictures show very morose, dull patients, but in my mother's before picture, she was hardly morose. She had bothered to put on makeup and jewelry; she looked tense but her eyes had a liveliness to them.

On Freeman's advice, on the following Monday, my mother was taken to Cedar Croft Sanitarium. My father reported that according to Freeman, my mother had

> what is known as dementia praecox [a term no longer in use, now called schizophrenia; in his own notes Freeman called her schizophrenia paranoid] he recommended the only known aid for this type—a surgical operation to sever nerve tissue connections with that part of the brain which stores up the excessive fears, suspicions, doubts, etc. The operation is relatively simple and safe, and often highly successful although no guarantee can be given. Beneficial effects are not apparent for several weeks, but at the end of six weeks, they should become noticeable. The operation was performed today—Monday—by Dr. Freeman.

My mother just before the lobotomy

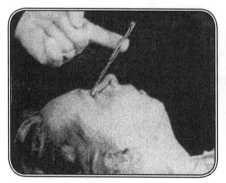 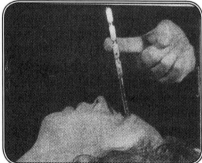

My mother during the lobotomy

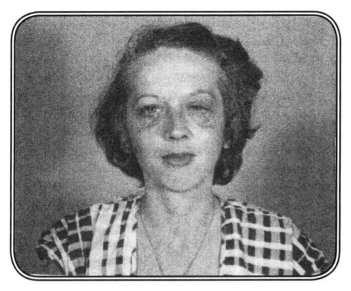

My mother soon after the lobotomy

On that day, July 17, 1950, with my mother giving her permission—which would be inadmissible today—Freeman performed a transorbital lobotomy on her. It was a procedure he devised in which he inserted an ice pick–like device through the thin bone in each eye orbital and swished it back and forth to cut nerve connections between the frontal lobes and the thalamus.

According to his description, Freeman would start by giving one to six electroshocks every two minutes to knock the patient out. The nose and mouth would be covered with a towel, and the point of the leucotome, Freeman's term for the ice pick device he used, was aimed underneath the upper eyelid with the shaft of the leucotome parallel with the bony center of the nose. A hammer was used to drive the leucotome through the orbital bone. He would then maneuver this instrument in various directions to make the cuts.[14] This was done with no imaging of the inside of the skull. Freeman could literally not see exactly what he was doing. He cut the neural fibers at various depths in his procedure; his medical records for my mother indicate he cut "deep."

All four people at the Cedar Croft Sanitarium that day thought they were doing the right thing. Freeman believed he was doing good and providing relief to my mother from painful fears and anguish. My grandmother Nana hoped that the lobotomy would deal with her daughter's "sexual perversion." My mother had consented to the operation in an obviously desperate attempt to win her husband back and out of guilt over her mother's hospitalization, which she felt she had caused. My father saw it as something to try, particularly I am sure as it was inexpensive compared to psychiatric care, and he thought of it as relatively harmless: "One cannot expect an operation to change a person's whole personality. In other words, she is apt to remain generally the same."

My father was wrong; lobotomies do change people's personalities; that is their function. Whether for better or worse is the issue. In fact, all four of those involved that day—Freeman, Nana, my mother, and my father—were dead wrong in doing what they did. My mother was at the center of a perfect storm. Society expected an ideal she could not fulfill. She had considerable stressors in her life including the physical pain she endured from her teeth extraction and her sore shoulder. She had been sexually frustrated, and her husband had just told her outright that he did not love her. Her mother had just been hospitalized for six weeks. At the same time, her mother was concerned about her masturbating and the possibility of promiscuity. My father wanted a less troublesome wife. Then came Freeman holding out the hope of a quick, inexpensive fix. It did not work.

Chapter 12

The Lobotomy Craze and Walter Freeman

For a long time in the twentieth century, the distinction between psychiatry and neurology was blurred. The American Neurological Association and the American Psychiatric Association existed, but according to Freeman, many of the top people in the two fields were members of both.[15] In the early 1930s, Freeman became one of the founders of the American Board of Psychiatry and Neurology and had the task of certifying individuals in psychiatry or neurology or in some cases both.[16]

The idea of cutting the connection between the frontal lobes and the thalamus to deal with mental illness had grown out of an international meeting of neurologists in London in 1935. Sitting on the board that organized the International Neurological Congress was Portuguese neurologist Egas Moniz, and among the four topics selected for discussion was the function of the frontal lobes.[17] The meeting was well attended; it drew participants from twenty countries including I. P. Pavlov from Russia.[18] Walter Freeman was a participant though at that time, frontal lobes were not his area of interest. He did however strike up a friendship with Moniz that lasted until the latter's death.

Among the papers presented was one by two Yale University neurologists who had conducted experiments giving ever more complex tasks to two chimpanzees. In the face of difficulties, one of the chimpanzees became extremely frustrated while the other remained docile. The neurologists then removed the frontal lobes of the chimpanzees and found that the operation did not affect the chimpanzees' cognitive abilities but did have an effect on their temperaments. The one that had become frustrated became docile, and the reverse occurred for the other.[19] According to Freeman, Moniz asked one of the Yale neurologists whether the removal of the frontal lobes might work for human beings and learned it was "highly improbable."[20]

Nevertheless, back in Lisbon, Moniz experimented on mental patients by injecting ethyl alcohol into the frontal lobes to temporarily block neural pathways. He soon, however, arranged for the performance of what he called a leucotomy on twenty severely mentally ill patients. A neurosurgeon colleague carried out the procedure, which involved puncturing two holes on either side of the skull and introducing a metal tube eleven centimeters long and two millimeters in diameter with a retractable wire loop at the end with which they made lesions in the brain. There was no removal of brain matter. Moniz quickly circulated his results without, as he said, waiting for follow-up and definitive results. He considered seven of the patients "cured clinically," seven "considerably improved," and six "in the same state."[21] The monograph spurred a worldwide interest in the procedure. Moniz was later to receive the Nobel Prize for Medicine or Physiology in 1949.

No matter what we think of lobotomies today, it is only fair to emphasize that at that time, there were no drugs to treat mental illness. The first antipsychotic, chlorpromazine, known commonly by its trade name Thorazine, was not readily available to psychiatrists in the United States until 1954.[22] The options available to those treating the mentally ill were limited. Aside from talk therapy that would not have been effective for the severely mentally ill, many were extreme from today's point of view. They included electroshock therapy, insulin-induced comas, hydrotherapy during which the patient was subjected to alternating hot and cold blasts of water,[23] and various forms of psychosurgery.[24]

There were no ethics committees scrutinizing research before allowing it to proceed. Experimentation on humans was not generally frowned upon. The most horrific example of course was the Nazis' use of concentration camp prisoners in various experiments that often led to death. As their defense at the Nuremburg war crimes trials, the doctors who performed such experiments argued that there was no difference between their experiments and those done on inmates in US prisons.[25]

Further, the US Public Health Service itself carried out between 1932 and 1972 a study of the effects of untreated syphilis on poor, male, African-American sharecroppers in

Alabama. The participants were told they would receive free health care from the government, but they were never told they had syphilis, nor were they given penicillin after it was discovered.[26] It is a shameful blot on our history.

Lobotomies were clearly experimental. Scientists had two aims each laudable in itself but together potentially dangerous. One was to provide relief to the mentally ill, and the other was to find out just what function the frontal lobes actually performed. Why did a lobotomy provide the relief it seemed to provide in some patients? The first aim required a very humane point of view, but the second demanded a very detached, clinical perspective. The first was vulnerable to being overridden by the second.

Like Moniz, Freeman was a neurologist with the neurologist's focus on physical causes of mental illness. He was serving on the faculty and in the hospital run by George Washington University in Washington, DC, when he read Moniz's paper. He had, however, previously been in charge of the laboratory at Washington's largest public hospital for the mentally ill, St. Elizabeths, and he had seen the terrible toll mental illness could take particularly on World War I veterans who were "shell shocked"; the term *posttraumatic stress disorder* was not used until the Vietnam War.

Freeman soon formed a partnership with a colleague at George Washington University, a neurosurgeon named James W. Watts, and they performed their first lobotomy (and the first lobotomy in the United States) in the fall of 1936. They called it a *lobotomy* to differentiate the instrument and procedure they used from those of Moniz. While Moniz made lesions, Freeman and Watts cut the neural fibers connecting the frontal lobes to the rest of the brain.

They tried different techniques at first, but the one on which they settled came to be called the standard lobotomy. The patient's scalp was shaved and cleansed, and the patient's head was placed on a sandbag with the head slightly elevated above the feet. Often, only a local anesthetic was administered. The "*approximate* location of the coronal suture" (italics mine) would be marked with a violet dye. The coronal suture is a seam across the skull where the frontal and the parietal bones meet. Watts would mark and drill burr holes on this line on each side of the head; into these he inserted the cutting device, a blunt, narrow knife about fifteen centimeters long. With Freeman serving as guide, Watts waggled the cutting instrument back and forth to cut the neural fibers.[27] That was obviously hardly an exact procedure.

Watts and Freeman famously failed in the case of Rosemary Kennedy, the daughter of Joseph Kennedy. She had a below-average IQ to begin with, and she was beginning to be rebellious and unruly. In secret, her father had Watts and Freeman operate on her with disastrous results that led to her being practically a vegetable. She was secluded, and no word of this incident got out to the public at the time.[28]

In their 1942 publication *Psychosurgery: Intelligence and Social Behavior Following Prefrontal Lobotomy for Mental Disorders*, Freeman and Watts reported on their work with some eighty patients, sixty-one females and nineteen males. These were generally presented as case studies— detailed descriptions of the patients before and after surgery along with before-and-after photographs. Freeman and Watts were clearly experimenting to find out how deep they had to cut to affect the relief they sought, to find out which illnesses were best suited for a lobotomy (it had no beneficial effect, for example, for alcoholics), and to document behavior after the surgery and what effects they considered temporary and permanent. Finally, they give their theory about the function of the frontal lobes.

In their preface, Freeman and Watts stated,

> Operations upon the brain are by no means to be applied indiscriminately in the treatment of functional mental disorders. In fact, in view of certain unfortunate results, the operation of prefrontal lobotomy is reserved for those patients whose outlook for recovery is poor, whose response to other treatment is unsatisfactory and for those who are facing disability or suicide.[29]

Later, they added,

> The effects of the operation have by no means always been entirely for the good; it seems quite certain that an individual wishing to be relieved of certain distressing symptoms has to pay a certain price. The families also have to pay a certain price for such relief and must be willing and able to cooperate to a certain degree in handling the postoperative deficiencies that occur in these patients.[30]

The aftereffects patients had varied and could include epileptic seizures and death. Basically, however, a lobotomy reduced a patient to childishness, a general dullness of personality, and a lack of forethought and initiative.[31] There was also a general lack of tact; they would sometimes speak too frankly and aggressively.[32]

Between the publication of this book and the second edition, which appeared in 1950, the year my mother received her lobotomy, there was a massive proliferation of lobotomies performed in this country and overseas. A big impetus came after World War II when the Veterans Administration was faced with the underbelly of war—the men who did not return to the American Dream but instead to terrible mental suffering and often unmanageable behavior.

Two VA doctors witnessed one of Freeman's and Watts's lobotomies and recommended it as a relatively simple procedure in a report to the head of the VA, who in short order approved its use in hopes of reducing the number of veterans who had to be institutionalized. With Freeman and Watts acting as consultants, between the spring of 1947 and the fall of 1950, about 2,000 veterans in some fifty VA hospitals across the nation were lobotomized.[33]

From the beginning, Freeman and Watts faced substantial criticism from members of the medical community. There was opposition to the idea of mutilating the brain and undertaking surgery on the brain before other, less drastic measures had been tried.[34] They were unable to secure foundation grants,[35] and even St. Elizabeths Hospital in DC, where Freeman had worked, eventually refused to allow him to remain as a consultant.[36]

Likewise, within the VA were many psychiatrists who were critical and saw Freeman as a loose cannon proposing lobotomies for just about anything.[37] For many years, however, the criticism was kept mainly in communications among professionals and not widely known by the public. That was in part due to Freeman's aggressively taking his case for lobotomies to the public. He was a showman who loved the limelight. He even wrote an article for the *Journal of Medical Education* called "Showmanship in Medical Teaching."[38]

Freeman craved attention. He greatly admired his maternal grandfather, William Keen Jr., who "reached international renown in the field of surgery"[39] and who helped secure opportunities for the young Freeman.[40] Later in life, Freeman opined, "I have waited in vain for an honorary degree, of which my grandfather had six or seven."[41]

Soon after he and Watts presented their first paper on the few lobotomies they had performed to a medical society and received considerable criticism, Freeman cultivated the popular press. Before appearing to speak at the next medical association, Freeman

> called Tom Henry, science writer for the *Washington Post,* had him come to George Washington University Hospital, explained what we were doing and what theories had been advanced, persuaded him to see patients before and after, and to witness an operation. I wanted to get an accurate account on record.

As was to be expected, there was considerable journalistic interest when Watts and I arrived in Baltimore [where the meeting was being held]. Chief place was taken by Alex Gifford, a Yale classmate of mine, who pursued me and tried to get the whole story.[42]

Freeman also made himself newsworthy through the exhibits he and Watts had at the various meetings where they presented papers. "I found the technic of getting noticed in the papers. It was to arrive a day or two ahead of the opening and install the exhibit in the most graphic manner and then be alert for prowling newsmen. I also made friends with science writers."[43]

As a consequence, the early uncritical praise of Freeman's work helped encourage the widespread popularity of lobotomies with other doctors. In 1946, approximately 500 lobotomies were performed, and by 1949, the number had risen to about 5,000 for the year.[44] Articles in popular publications of the time such as *The Saturday Evening Post*[45] portrayed a lobotomy as a precision procedure when in fact it was far from precise. The successes were dramatized, and short shrift was given to the failures and negative side effects.[46]

In addition, despite criticism within the medical community, Freeman published professional articles in prestigious journals such as the *American Journal of Psychiatry*, the *Journal of the American Medical Association*, the *Journal of Neuropathology and Experimental Neurology*, and a host of others domestic and international. For years, he wrote an annual review of research in the field of psychosurgery for the *American Journal of Psychiatry.*

Freeman and Watts parted ways in 1947 with Freeman's introduction of the transorbital lobotomy, the type of lobotomy described earlier that my mother underwent.[47] It had first been performed in Italy about a decade earlier.[48] In Freeman's view, transorbital lobotomies using an ice pick device through the eye socket brought relief to the masses. He felt that psychiatrists could handle the procedure in their offices, not just neurosurgeons in hospital settings, in about fifteen to twenty minutes and at a much lower cost than the standard lobotomy. It was quick, ten to fifteen minutes, and relatively cheap, about $250, compared to the cost of lengthy analysis or hospitalization at thousands per year.[49] He turned to trying transorbital lobotomies when he found the standard lobotomies "too damaging" after encountering "a number of dramatic instances of severe personality downgrading in well-preserved patients."[50]

As time passed, Freeman and others began to see transorbital lobotomies as the preferred first choice of treatment rather than the treatment of last resort. Freeman felt the earlier the better, and lobotomies began to be used for what was termed intractable physical pain, not just mental anguish. They were performed on patients with for example cancer, back pain,[51] and ulcerative colitis.[52]

Playing the role of evangelist for transorbital lobotomies, Freeman traveled the country giving demonstrations at those state mental institutions that would allow him to perform the procedure. In West Virginia, he put on a virtuoso performance by performing 228 lobotomies in twelve days.[53] In one afternoon, he performed lobotomies on thirty-five women.[54] "Pregnant patients presented no complications."[55]

At the time of the publication of the second edition of *Psychosurgery* in 1950, Freeman and Watts still collaborated on the first part of the book devoted to discussing the standard prefrontal lobotomy. Several things are striking in the second edition as compared to the first and have a direct bearing on my mother's case. In the latter edition, there are clearer statements of what the negative effects of lobotomies were.

> Inertia and lack of ambition, reduction in consecutive thinking, loss of what is commonly called self-consciousness, indifference to the opinions of others, satisfaction with performance even though this may be of inferior quality and quantity—these may be considered among the primary results.[56]

> There is some quality of imagination that is apparently reduced, and probably permanently.[57]

> Introspection, contemplation and philosophizing are no longer feasible.[58]

But the exact outcome for any individual patient could not be predicted. The case studies themselves reveal very different reactions. Freeman and Watts estimated that about a third of the cases were successful, that is, the patient could be out in the world working. Another third were considered "fair"; they could leave the institution and be at home but could not work. And about a third were failures; they did not respond to treatment and had to remain institutionalized. There was a death rate of about 3 percent, and about 1 percent were made worse by the procedure.[59]

The second edition of *Psychosurgery* also emphasized much more strongly the role that the family had to play in the recovery of patients from the standard prefrontal lobotomy.

> We make it very clear to the relatives that we expect them to carry out the program of convalescent care; in fact, unless the relatives will make suitable arrangement—and this may include moving to a larger home or engaging the services of competent aides—we decline to operate.[60]

> It is no easy job that the family has on its hands in bringing the patient back to useful existence following prefrontal lobotomy. The convalescence is long and tedious, marked by many crises of various sorts, and only an abiding will to succeed will restore the patient to adequate social function in the family environment.[61]

I was obviously not in the room when Freeman spoke to my father, grandmother, and mother about the procedure. But from my father's letters, it appears that the negative side effects and possible dangers were not discussed or at least not stressed, nor was the major, long-term role the family would need to play in recovery. My father thought my mother would get better or remain the same.

Some hint of what Freeman might have said, however, is in the short section of the second edition of *Psychosurgery* called "Results of Transorbital Lobotomy." Freeman alone wrote it, and it had a decidedly different tone and portrayal of outcomes than did the rest of the book. Freeman stated, "Recovery from transorbital lobotomy is spectacular ... they [the patients] are encouraged to return home the day following operation and to resume their tasks as soon as the discoloration about their eyes clears up."[62] No mention of family involvement, no mention of negative side effects except that relapses often occurred, which he suggested might be treated by electroshock therapy.

> These patients recover without any apparent personality deficit, although for a few weeks there may be a certain lack of subtlety in their relationships with other people. They often made a superior adjustment, even in the recreational or social welfare stage ... There is no long-drawn-out convalescence with requirements for retraining, although there are often echo symptoms that are slow in clearing up, sometimes requiring months to disappear.[63]

Freeman was wrong at least in the case of my mother in his almost manic optimism about the treatment.

Freeman himself had a mental health issue. In 1933, he suffered from what he termed a "nervous breakdown."

I was completing my book on neuropathology, working on that from 4 to 7 am. Then came a full day as director of laboratories at St. Elizabeths Hospital, a drive through heavy traffic to my office to see patients until 7 or 8 pm and home to a wife who seemed to cough all night, while outside the streetcars pounded along Connecticut Avenue, their wheels poorly kept up during the Depression. Sleep would not come. I grew irritable, morbid and depressed.[64]

A trip to Europe eventually lifted his spirits, and he felt he had learned from the experience how hard he could push himself, what the early symptoms were, and what he could do to counteract them.[65] The possibility followed him through his life. "I may have skirted the edge on some occasions, when I was close to the breaking point, but I recognized insomnia as my first danger signal and protected myself against it by nembutal [an addictive barbiturate now used in euthanasia and executions]."[66] He took it every night for some thirty years and admitted to being dependent on it, but he did not consider himself addicted.[67]

For a professional in his field, Freeman sometimes displayed rather rash, impulsive behavior.

I was the first in Washington to use convulsive shock therapy in the treatment of mental disorders. During the war [World War II] it was almost impossible to give it in the hospital, so I started it as an office procedure. It was before the days of the use of muscle relaxants ... and

I had my share of fractures of various bones. I usually had my secretary assist me, or a member of the family, but in this case, a woman who had undergone a series of treatments by me several years previously, had suffered another attack of depression. Her husband had a bad heart, and my secretary refused to assist me so I gave the treatment alone. Most unfortunately, on the first convulsion the lady suffered fracture of both humeri. This was early in the morning. I gave her an injection of morphine and left her too soon to see some patients at the hospital. When I returned the fat was in the fire. The woman was writhing in pain and her husband was outraged. I called an orthopedist friend and had her admitted to the hospital.[68]

Freeman ended up with a lawsuit for which he admitted there were "no extenuating circumstances," and he settled out of court. "I had taken similar chances before, but this taught me the lesson that reasonable precautions must be used, and that no patient should be left in distress."[69]

He chose to include in the second edition of *Psychosurgery* a truly horrifying, full-page photograph of a thin, naked woman being strong-armed by two burly nurses to have a lobotomy.[70] In commenting on some of his papers, he stated, "How far off base I was in some of the more fanciful papers, I don't know, but I'm pretty sure that my chairman's address on psychochemistry, and a later one on Human Sonar were pretty far afield."[71]

He gave demonstrations of lobotomies using no mask or gloves. He gave my mother a lobotomy in less than three days of having met her, and during the summer he was treating her, he suffered what he termed a "minor stroke." But while in the hospital, he continued to treat patients there making rounds in his bathrobe.[72]

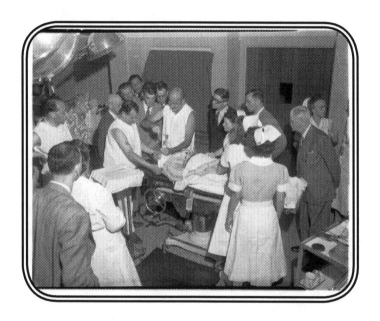

MOHAI, *Seattle Post-Intelligencer* Collection, 1986.5.25616

In 1949, criticism of lobotomies started to appear in the popular press.[73] The article entitled "Lobotomy Disappointment" from the December 12, 1949 edition of *Newsweek* reported on a meeting of the Washington, DC Psychiatric Society, of which Freeman was once president, in which lobotomies were severely criticized. Dr. Nolan D. C. Lewis, director of the New York State Psychiatric Institute of Columbia-Presbyterian Medical Center, outlined three complaints: lobotomies were being used without patients having the opportunity to recover by more conventional means, the procedure was being performed without there being any psychiatric examination, and there was too little follow-up to justify the claims made. He wondered whether the quieting of the patient was just a convenience for the caretakers.

Watts, who was present at the meeting, tried to defend the procedure, but several more psychiatrists spoke up about the far from splendid results at their own institutions.[74] At that time, the *New York Times, Scientific American*, and the *Nation* among others also carried articles voicing serious concerns.[75]

Freeman eventually responded to the critics in 1953 with an article in the *New England Journal of Medicine* entitled "Ethics of Psychosurgery." He argued the position of an earlier psychosurgeon who had hypothesized that there were two types of doctors—those who adopted the approach of *primum no nocere* (First, do no harm) and those who believed in *melius anceps remedium quam nullium* (It is better to do something rather than nothing—my translation).[76] "Patients are selected for leucotomy [he reverted to Moniz's term there] from the residue when others fail."[77] That was certainly not the case with my mother.

With the criticism of lobotomies mounting and the advent of psychoactive drugs, the number of lobotomies being performed dwindled. But Freeman kept on arguing for them suggesting that they might be a useful prelude to more in-depth talk therapy.[78] And he continued to perform lobotomies around the country where he was permitted to do so. It was not until 1967, long after Freeman had retired to California, that he performed his last lobotomies. He did two on the same day. One he considered successful; in the other, the patient died. Those were his last lobotomies.[79]

As I reflect on what happened to my mother, I feel anger toward Freeman for being so sure of the rightness of a lobotomy for my mother, but I also feel particular anger toward my father. I do not feel that toward my grandmother. She thought my father "very brilliant" and would have deferred to him. She had a 6th grade education; he had a college degree.

Although he no longer loved my mother, I believe my father had a moral responsibility to learn more about the procedure to which he was subjecting her. His letters show he knew something about electroshock therapy. He was a journalist used to delving into topics and asking questions. In his Air Bulletins, he made sure the medical information was accurate. He had a sister who was the future head reference librarian at the University of Chicago and who could have found him material to read. Criticisms of the procedure had begun to appear in the popular press. Even if he had read the first edition of *Psychosurgery*, he would have known about the possible results and dangers of lobotomies. And I wonder why he did not consult an actual psychiatrist. He never referred to Freeman as a psychiatrist, only as a "specialist".

As mentioned earlier, my father had gone to college in Baldwin City, Kansas, less than an hour from the Menninger Clinic in Topeka, Kansas. It was providing training for psychiatrists and psychologists from the 1930s on while my father was living in Baldwin.

In 1946, the Menninger School of Psychiatry was formed, and it became the largest training center for psychiatrists in the country. He might have contacted them for assistance in finding a psychiatrist in the Washington area for my mother. Instead, he somehow chose Freeman. Freeman's option certainly was cheaper than talk therapy, and it meant my father could avoid delving into topics and emotions he may have wanted to avoid.

But from my point of view, it was the major moral failure of my father's life and ran counter to the values he subsequently taught me. I do not know if learning about the effects would have changed his mind, but I fervently hope that would have been the case. I do know it might have made my mother's subsequent behavior more understandable to her family.

Chapter 13

The Immediate Aftermath

On the day she was lobotomized, my mother was thirty-three. I was going on seven, and Ricky was going on three. I do not remember visiting her at the sanitarium, but apparently, we went out to see her "about every other day. She isn't at all well yet, but then the specialist said that no improvement would show before about six weeks."

Freeman and the sanitarium staff were willing for my mother to come home right away, and she was anxious to return also. My father and grandmother, however, "felt very strongly that her coming home would be a mistake, and extremely hard upon all of us." My father told Freeman that he and Nana "could not take responsibility for her at present," so Freeman had my mother stay for ten more days. He would check on her and "If necessary, he said, he would perform another operation."

Meanwhile, my father, feeling that my mother would probably "remain generally the same," began pursuing two courses of action—having my mother institutionalized and legally separating from her, a difficult matter in Maryland, which had been founded as a Catholic colony.

By September 1, my mother was out of the sanitarium; we were all staying at a cottage on Chesapeake Bay where we had gone so many times to play in the sand and ocean. To his credit, my father was willing to commute about a hundred miles a day.

> Gretchen is somewhat better, but not in perfect condition by any means. However, she seems to enjoy it out at the Bay. Mrs. Richard plans to stay here until Robbie starts to school ... and then go to Dubuque for two or three weeks.

> Gretchen still has some very definite weaknesses in her thinking and emotional outlook, but she seems to have none of the very terrible ideas that she had formerly—at least she doesn't express them outwardly. Of course, one cannot expect a miracle from the operation, all one can say at the present is that there has been some improvement. Time will tell.

His mother's reaction to the news was moralistic—Gretchen needed to "square up" to common responsibilities with less self-centeredness.

I do not remember my mother being so much different after the operation except that she did spend a lot of time by herself. She sunbathed on a shelf of flat rocks while Ricky and I went collecting sharks' teeth on the shoreline or used sticks to toss out of the water the stinging jellyfish that plagued us when we went in.

But all was not well. Nana reported that Gretchen told her that a man in a grocery store "made a signal to her with a bunch of carrots." She also thought that the Korean War had been caused by her marital problems. When she entered Independence Mental Health Institute, my mother reported that she felt fine after the lobotomy.

> I didn't have any trouble that I started. I tried to make a go of it. My mother had to step in one night. I was in the bathroom with my little son, and my husband came in and grabbed me and threw me out, and then said that I had done something to harm my boy sexually. I wouldn't do anything like that. I am a mother.

I kicked him and said now I know who has the
evil mind. And he said, I will kill you yet.

My brother and I have discussed this incident; he certainly
does not believe our mother molested him particularly as she
emphatically stated that she was a mother. Everyone seemed
to have been on edge particularly with anything that had to
do with sex. As my father said, "It isn't just what she actually
does or says that exhausts one physically and mentally; it's
also the anxiety over what she might do." They were looking
for failure and not providing the kind of support a lobotomy
patient needed whether or not Freeman thought it was
necessary for transorbital lobotomy patients.

Mom photographed by Freeman in August

I started school that fall, but not at Riverdale, where I had gone to first grade. The number of us new suburban kids strained the capacity of the local schools. Instead, I was bused along with others from my neighborhood to Greenbelt Elementary School. After I started school, Nana went back to Dubuque to take care of matters there. She had wanted to take my mother with her, and my mother wanted to go, but Nana knew that my mother would not go without us kids and that my father would not permit that. He knew from his lawyer that it would be tantamount to saying that Gretchen was competent to take care of us. Nana planned to be away for several weeks and then return to Hyattsville.

In the meantime, however, my mother decided to take matters into her own hands. As part of the craziness of the whole situation, while my father was not willing to let my mother take us to Dubuque because it would signal she was capable of taking care of us, it was indeed my mother who took care of us in Hyattsville while my father worked.

One of the disabilities caused by a lobotomy is lack of foresight; my mother exhibited that as she put in motion her decision to pack up and leave for Dubuque. Life alone with my father must have been unbearable for her by then, and she must have wanted to flee that toxic environment. She also wanted me to go to Catholic school, which my father firmly opposed. My father reported that I also did not want to go to a Catholic school but to the school my friends attended— Greenbelt Elementary. My mother interpreted that as my father's turning me against the idea of Catholic school. What I actually thought I do not remember.

One morning, my mother told me that I was not going to school that day because she, Ricky and I were going on a trip. I was sent outside to play, but of course there was no one to play with, so I spent a lonely morning kicking stones around near the viaduct at the bottom of our street. My mother must have been packing, but when we got in the taxi, we did not have a lot of luggage.

We got to the train station and boarded a train. It turned out that my mother had not bought tickets; we kept moving from one car to the next as the conductor came through the cars to collect tickets. He caught up with us in the last car, the club car; I was nervous and embarrassed by it all, but my mother apparently had the money and paid him.

When we got to Chicago, she realized she had not left any message about our leaving for my father, so she rushed to send him a telegram. She did not, however, bother to inform her mother that we were coming.

My father reported the incident thusly to his mother.

> To make a long story short, Gretchen took the children to Dubuque by train on Tuesday. She gave no advance notice. I came home from work to find them gone. There was no note or anything so naturally I had a rather difficult time piecing together what had happened, especially since none of the neighbors said they had seen her leave. Late in the evening the Western Union called with a wire Gretchen had sent from the train, saying that she was ill and was going to Dubuque. Mrs. Richard

phoned me yesterday to say that they had arrived okay. I had called Mrs. Richard the night they left to find out if Gretchen had told her she was coming, but she had not. When I received the wire from Gretchen, I notified Mrs. Richard. Mrs. Richard was to have returned to Washington this Saturday.

In this letter, he sounds very matter of fact and does not seem worried about what was happening to Ricky and me much less our mother. Neither my father nor my grandmother was apparently aware of the lack of foresight a lobotomy could produce. Had they known, it may have made the incident more understandable and not just another manifestation of her mental illness.

Now began a terrible time for all concerned. My brother and I were back at the cold-water flat with no privacy, and my mother began to seriously deteriorate. The lobotomy had made her condition worse. She became obsessed with my being a "good girl" and started a system of awarding gold stars on a calendar when I was "good." I have no recollection of what that entailed. She also became obsessed with my bowel movements; if I did not have one every day, she would give me an enema. I truly hated and was frightened by her actions. I would sit on the toilet for long periods staring at the religious calendar on the backside of the door with pictures of the bleeding heart of Jesus and do my best to produce a bowel movement. The thought of lying about it did not occur to me—I was supposed to be a "good girl." To this day, I cannot stand the bleeding-heart plant as it reminds me of that time. I of course attended the Catholic school there.

My father reacted to the situation by making himself a victim. My mother's driving the car into a telephone pole had already been framed as an attack on him according to the college friend he had consulted. After having told my mother earlier that he did not love her anymore, my father wrote to his family projecting the lack of love onto my mother. "Until recently I always went on the assumption that my wife loved me, that the unhappiness and tension she created was caused by outside factors, by me especially … The fact of the matter is, of course, that my wife does not love me and is incapable of it."

My grandmother, however, bore the brunt. She was a widow with an apartment house to run and had to look after her sister, Martha, who had suffered a heart attack in 1947 and could not work. And her only surviving child had a disturbed mind. As a mother myself, I know that must have been devastating. In her case doubly so as Nana had had some injury before her marriage that made carrying a child to term very difficult. She had lost six children in childbirth or early infancy. Our mother was Nana's fourth pregnancy during which she stayed in bed almost the whole nine months. Even then, my mother was malnourished at first (she could not drink regular milk and had to be fed goat's milk) and was undersized until she was four. It is no wonder that Nana referred to my mother as "baby" in her first meeting with the mental institute staff. Her first question was, "Will I be able to see my baby?"

In the intake report to the mental institution, Nana stated that Gretchen had been having a lot of sexual problems. "She encouraged the mother to have sexual relations with her several times. She has overemphasized sexual matters while talking to other people. The mother is not aware that the patient went out with other men prior to her admission to this hospital." So there was a lot of talk but no actual promiscuousness. As my father was quoted earlier saying, "It isn't just what she actually does or says that exhausts one physically and mentally; it's also the anxiety over what she might do."

Otherwise, my mother spent her days doing some sewing. "At times, it seemed the patient were living in a dream world." Lack of initiative is another outcome of lobotomies. Although at one point my mother talked of getting a job, nothing came of it. In November, Gretchen had "some sort of spell." She had a headache that subsided, but then, she "suddenly talked very abusively to her mother. She accused her of not being a good mother and not allowing her to have an adequate sex life and that she hated her mother." Lobotomies loosen inhibitions; abusive speech is another outcome seen in lobotomy patients.

My mother reportedly felt that her marital difficulties had caused the Korean War, and she was occasionally afraid of Communists. "Her eyes appeared to be rather glassy at times and there is evidence that she had been having some relations with the little boy as his sex organs were rather discolored." Again, my brother and I have discussed this, and he does not accept my grandmother's surmise. She never actually saw anything happening and was hypersensitive to our mother's sexual speech. My brother researched whether a discolored scrotum was a sign of sexual abuse in males but found no evidence of that. In fact, babies can naturally have darker scrotums.

At that time, Nana and my father had been trying to work out what to do. Nana first planned to come to Washington alone, but my mother opposed that. Nana proposed to try to bring us all back to Hyattsville. "She said Gretchen was all mixed and we would probably 'have to put her away.'"

My father talked the situation over with his lawyer and wrote Nana that he thought it would be "bad to bring Gretchen here against her will, that Gretchen had decided to go out to Dubuque of her own free will." Everett saw that as an unbearable situation and no doubt was right. He also at that point resisted the idea of putting our mother away for Ricky's and my sakes. He felt it best that Gretchen remain in Dubuque even with us kids and go her own way for a while "since her present major upsets seem to center on me."

As expected, Pearl was quite critical of Gretchen. She wrote to Louis,

> The other time, she was often threatening to leave him and go there [Dubuque] and kept it up so finally after she wrecked the car, in her wish to baffle him, he just went ahead and had her go. Wonder if she and her mother are fighting each other again. It is a sad mess. I think it is willfulness and a desire to contrary and taunt him (with the Catholic element aggravating it) … Well I think these Catholics should marry

Catholics and not wreck other people's lives as well as their own.

Pearl was concerned that Gretchen not "be free to roam around she might get into trouble although I think it is more vanity that makes her want to flirt. How obnoxious."

I have no idea if my mother was flirting with men or if Pearl just assumed it given Gretchen's sexual talk. Pearl frowned on any sort of flirting. In a discussion with his mother and Christine while he was in college, my father had told Christine that she should flatter men more. Pearl retorted, "The trouble was young men takes it that they are being chased." It was for men to do the chasing.

In late October, Nana somehow was finally able to get away and come to Washington for three days to discuss things with my father. My father was hoping to get my mother into the federally run St. Elizabeths mental institution there, which had a good reputation, and he had his lawyer working on that.

That did not, however, happen immediately. His sister had sent him a train ticket to Chicago as a birthday gift, and he planned to use it after getting a free trip as a sort of representative of the State Department and delegate for the Washington, DC chapter to the professional journalists' society Sigma Delta Chi convention in Miami. He also got a promotion at work. He subsequently did use his train ticket; he spent Thanksgiving in Chicago with his family, but his letters give no indication that he met or talked with Nana at that time or came to see us kids. He referred only to how relaxing it was to be with his folks.

In a letter dated December 3, 1950, my father stated that Nana did not like the idea of Gretchen's being hospitalized in Dubuque and wanted her to be institutionalized in Maryland. The plan worked out was to try to have Gretchen come to Washington by car with some friends to pick up her clothes and other items. If she came, Freeman would make arrangements for her institutionalization there. If she didn't, Freeman would put Nana in touch with a psychiatrist in Dubuque who could help arrange temporary institutionalization and Freeman would arrange for the transfer to Washington later. Our father would then come to Dubuque to get us.

None of that elaborate trap happened. What happened next definitely questions the assumption that Nana and my father were truly coordinating their efforts. That is because sometime in November, Nana applied to have my mother declared insane and institutionalized in Iowa. Meanwhile, on December 6, she was so concerned about Gretchen that she had her hospitalized at St. Joseph Sanitarium, where my mother had previously received electroshock therapy.

Adjudging someone insane is a legal process. The court records for my mother are sealed. The general procedure in Iowa at the time, however, was for an individual (it did not have to be a relative) to fill out an application stating his or her belief that the respondent—the supposedly mentally ill individual—was "seriously mentally impaired." That, accompanied by a written statement in support of the applicant by a licensed physician and one or more supporting affidavits from other observers, was submitted to the clerk of the district court. A time and place for a hearing before the district court would then be set. The respondent would receive a copy of the notice concerning the hearing and could hire an attorney.

Prior to the hearing on hospitalization, one or more licensed physicians would examine the respondent and submit a written report or reports. The respondent could have an examination by a physician of his or her own choice to be submitted in evidence. My mother was in no condition to respond to the court proceedings.

After undergoing this process, my mother was "adjudged insane" on January 9, 1951, and admitted to the Independence Mental Health Institute in Independence, Iowa, one of four such facilities in Iowa; it was about an hour's drive west of Dubuque. As discussed in the next chapter, Nana was not in Dubuque at the time of the examination and judgment or for the transfer from St. Joseph's Sanitarium to Independence Mental Health Institute. My mother must have been very confused and frightened about what was happening to her. Someone who was a stranger, perhaps from the sheriff's department, would have had the responsibility of taking her there from St. Joseph's.

Earlier in December, as soon as my father knew that Gretchen was in St. Joseph's, he telegrammed his mother to meet him at the train station in Chicago ready to accompany him to Dubuque. He picked Ricky and me up, and we landed back in Hyattsville with no one to look after us initially except a kindly neighbor who kept an eye on us.

I thus changed schools yet again, returning to Greenbelt Elementary, and I had no mother. I was by that time close to being a feral child. I would not comb my hair; on weekends, my father would try to get what he called the "rat's nest" out of my fine hair. I refused to wipe myself, and I masturbated as I pleased by squeezing my legs together (and yes, I achieved orgasm). The adult world had failed me, and I was totally angry at being shuffled about like a sack of potatoes. Everyone talked about taking action for the sake of the children, but I saw no one caring about what was going on inside me. That was to continue throughout that year.

Chapter 14

Pearl Comes to Hyattsville

In 1951, I turned eight. It was another awful year for me as well as my mother. My father obviously needed help caring for Ricky and me. Thus, sometime after committing Gretchen to St. Joseph's, Nana came to Hyattsville to look after us. She and my father were surprised in January when they learned that the judgment of insanity for which Nana had petitioned in November had occurred and that my mother had already been transferred to the nearest state mental facility. Almost immediately after my mother's transfer, the Independence Mental Health Institute sent my father a survey gathering information about my mother that he returned on January 15.

Subsequent to their receiving his answers, a physician at the institute took my mother's history and gave her a physical examination on February 7, 1951. In his summary, the doctor stated,

> This patient is well oriented in all spheres, seems to be well backed up with her past life. Retention and immediate recall very good.

Information received about her past life from her has been fairly well established. She is uncertain as to what the outcome of her life will be. She has some paranoid ideas in regard to her husband and she is no doubt experiencing some persecutory ideas.

That is a rather placid report with no sense of my mother's condition warranting anywhere near the level of concern Nana had expressed.

Nana cared for Ricky and me until February 20, when she returned to Dubuque. The Institute had written her that they needed her to return for an in-person interview. On February 22, Nana made a detailed statement at the facility about family history, personal history, education, industrial (work history), personality, previous illness, religion, marital history, and present illness. The staff comment was that "She [Nana] appeared to be quite emotional in the worker's office. She also expressed some anxiety and possibly is somewhat over anxious." When Nana left Hyattsville, the plan was for her to return in about a month to look after us, but circumstances eventually changed that plan. She never returned.

The person who came to look after my brother and me in Hyattsville was our Grandmother Pearl. She arrived just before Nana left for Dubuque. It was supposed to be a temporary assignment, but it ended up lasting a little over a year until Pearl's death.

Pearl had somewhat fragile health as a child; her mother, who had a teaching certificate, had homeschooled her, so living on a farm, she did not have the companionship of classmates. She spent a good part of her twenties in various teaching positions. Pearl had had some training for being a teacher and had taught two years in Barrett, Kansas, where she met her future husband, Louis, probably at one of the many Methodist meetings and events they attended. Each was deeply involved in the church and held local leadership positions.

Pearl taught at five schools around Kansas. She and Louis corresponded a great deal during their courtship and engagement. At the time of her first letter to Louis in January 1908, she was leaving her current teaching position because "the doctor told me there was no other way to prevent a breakdown as I had nervous chills." She was then almost thirty-two, and Louis was almost thirty-seven.

The next school year, she taught at Bigelow, Kansas, until she had to return home to help with her dying mother. Her mother was a lively writer of letters that local newspapers printed. She wrote about her experiences as a schoolteacher, which at the time was a lonely position subject to scrutiny and criticism from all sides in whatever community the teacher was hired. "There is nothing under the sun a poor, 'lone, lorn' woman in the country *can* do but teach school (or get married,) and she must be very meek and conciliatory if she gets to do *that*—which includes the phrase in parenthesis." Her mother was obviously outspoken with a good sense of humor; Pearl was outspoken but had no sense of humor.

By the time of her correspondence with Louis, all Pearl's siblings but one were married, and after her mother's death, she was keeping house for her father and brother. The farm she had grown up on was rented out, and she was living in the town of Onaga. Her brother and father were busy with their own concerns and not much company. She was deeply lonely. That theme is unrelenting in all her letters to Louis. She said in one letter,

> I wish I had company more for when one is alone so much they think more than is good for them. If one could talk over things with someone it wouldn't wear on them so and I feel sometimes as if I would have to have a change but I pray for strength to take me through without failing.

She realized that her loneliness was probably making her sick. She suffered constantly from migraines that developed one month after her engagement to Louis on April 10, 1910, and she had another episode of "nervous chills" on the anniversary of her mother's death.

Pearl obviously longed to share a closeness with someone of a like mind, and she much admired Louis as a good, upstanding Methodist: "I have liked other young men too, but never anyone as I care for you. There is a great deal of difference and I am thankful I waited for my ideal and kept a high standard."

Louis was recuperating from a very debilitating illness involving his lungs that left him underweight and easily tired. They corresponded so much because they were seldom together and as a consequence really did not know each other. Louis was slow and cautious in making plans while Pearl had a nervous disposition and was constantly full of plans she wanted to see put in action, although most rarely were.

Louis's illness was the reason he kept giving for not making the trip from his family's farm in Frankfort to visit her in Onaga, a distance of some twenty-nine miles. It took him over a year from the date of their engagement to finally make it to her home and meet her father. Many a woman would have wondered about his commitment, and there were friends of hers who did. Having known my grandfather and his deliberate and slow ways, I do not think he lacked commitment to her at the time, but he had a far more comfortable life in his home than Pearl had in hers.

His father had died when he was one; his mother, two sisters, and three brothers had brought him up. Theirs was a very supportive and close-knit family that had not dispersed as Pearl's had. They managed a large and prosperous farm with all sharing in the proceeds. Pearl later commented to Christine that Louis had been spoiled, a trait on the list of her cardinal sins.

Despite his dragging his feet first over visiting her and then over setting a wedding date, Louis and Pearl married on February 4, 1913, some three years after their engagement. She was thirty-five and Louis was forty. They settled on a farm near the Reb homestead. Pearl then had to face the reality of sex, which she disliked; she thought it was basically a barnyard exercise.

Louis was not a talkative or assertive man particularly with his older siblings, and the companionship she had expected to stave off loneliness was just not there. Her adulation of him turned sour. In fact, she dominated and castigated him regularly. He was to bitterly complain to one of his brothers, "Sometimes she goes so far she doesn't leave me anything to lean on, but God ..."

The role of confidant was filled by her daughter Christine, who was born in 1914, a little over a year after the marriage. Pearl simply adored Christine ("I want you so badly ..." "Dearly Beloved"), and when Christine eventually left home to pursue graduate work in library science and her career, Pearl was frantic about the loss of immediate contact. She wrote to Christine almost every other day and expected the same in return. In fact, she desired daily letters. She wanted to know every little detail about Christine's life including what Christine ate and wore, what she spent her money on, and how she handled her laundry. Pearl constantly suggested plans for them to be together. My aunt did get angry with her mother at times and managed to set boundaries to her mother's intrusions without losing affection for her mother. She did not, however, marry until late in life, after her parents had died.

When my father was born in 1918, four years after Christine, Pearl did not develop the same emotional bond with him. Though Pearl was proud of his accomplishments, he was always second best to Christine.

During the Depression, Pearl and Louis lost two farms and their hard life became even harder. She enfolded herself more in Methodism; her social life centered on that. She and Louis attended church and other events together but were more like ships passing in the night. As she wrote Christine, "He seems so very lacking in the ways that give a feeling of concern [for her] ... It's his ego." She said that in the face of the nice things he did for her such as baking her a birthday cake and doing the washing and "kitchen work" when her legs were bothering her.

She could be sharply critical of people who did not follow what she considered the correct path. "What is Roberta Allen's [not me] husband doing and why does she take library training instead of keeping house?" Housekeeping was the job of married women period. Pearl became judgmental and a meddler in her family's life. She never seemed to doubt she was always right.

Pearl was the wrong person for the job of caring for Ricky and me, but to her credit, she knew that. She was seventy-three and plagued by leg sores, which she had had for well over twenty years due to extremely high blood pressure. Unlike Nana, who was subject to blood clots and listened to her doctors, Pearl distained doctors; she felt all they were after was her money. She preferred her own home remedies such as applying Listerine to the sores, which of course did not work. When she arrived in Hyattsville, a maid came several times a week to take care of household chores. Pearl at first appreciated her particularly as the maid was willing to look after us kids and give Pearl a rest, but later, Pearl decided she should do without this help even though it made her life easier. When she caught bronchitis, she refused to let my father call a doctor. She was determined to be a martyr. She was not going to be "self-centered" even if her life depended on it, and it did. I do not think the word *fun* existed in her vocabulary.

Once Pearl arrived in Hyattsville, we saw little of our father; he was content to leave us in her care. I suspect he wanted to avoid her given all that had occurred in his childhood and the constant suggestions she would have made about what was to be done. He went to a friend's house for dinner shortly after Pearl arrived and spent a great deal of his free time finishing off the upstairs of our house into two bedrooms, which we sorely needed, with the help of neighbors and friends. That was an ongoing project for most of the year.

Later in the year, he decided to take French classes on a weekday night at the Library of Congress. He also had to work at his office on certain Saturdays. In the course of the year, Ricky started to show the effects of my father's absence in his life. He began to give my father trouble according to Pearl, and he cried when my father left the house.

I do not remember my father's absence affecting me that way. We at least enjoyed Sundays with him, attending church when we were able, eating out at a restaurant chain called Hot Shoppes, going for a drive, taking in the cherry blossoms around the reflective pool in front of the Lincoln Memorial, and visiting the Smithsonian, or some other cultural institution.

My grandmother Pearl was much for excursions and planning longer trips with all the family members including Christine and Louis. In her mind, most of these activities except for picnics would have been for "educational" purposes, not for pure enjoyment. I did enjoy them though I intensely disliked her.

When Nana left for Dubuque, Pearl wrote Christine and Louis, "Robbie felt pretty lonesome and wanted me to sleep with her and seems OK today." Within two days, however, I was presenting problems in Pearl's eyes.

> Robbie can be nice but is quite willful and contrary and of course has been babied by Mrs. R [Nana] and dominated too, so she is quite difficult at times which spoils things some. Of course one feels sorry for her, with the situation as it has been, but she needs to develop another

"line" and I've concluded to be a little "plain" about it.

I couldn't have been all that terrible; she reported in the same letter that when she tumbled as a result of stepping on toys on the floor, "Robbie brot [*sic*] me a wet cloth (which I appreciated!)" But all in all, we were off to a bad start, and it got worse.

Chapter 15

My Mother at Independence Mental Health Institute

Meanwhile, my mother was at Independence Mental Health Institute along with 1,632 other patients and 311 employees.[80] The stereotypical image of a mental institution is grim and close to that of a prison, but Independence Mental Health Institute seemed hardly a grim place. There were and are no fences or bars on windows, only beautifully landscaped grounds that cover hundreds of acres.

The curving drive up to the main building is like driving up to an estate. It was built on the Kirkbride system, which involved following very definite specifications for almost every aspect of the buildings as well as the type of activities and care patients should receive.[81] The main building, the lofty administrative section with an ornate mansard roof, had wards off to each side, one for females and one for males.[82]

Thomas Kirkbride had been very influential when the facility was being built in the 1870s. He believed that the mentally ill should be treated humanely, according to the Golden Rule, and that the vast majority could be cured in the proper institutional setting.[83]

Part of the cure involved surrounding them with beautiful things and stimulating activities. The greenhouse at Independence grew flowers for beautifying the grounds and providing fresh bouquets for every ward.[84] They staged events such as concerts given by the Institute's band made up of patients for members of the Independence community in a stunning stained-glass auditorium. Soon after my mother's arrival, she participated in a minstrel show for which she also helped make the costumes. In fact, Kirkbride regarded nightly entertainments put on by patients as extremely important along with intellectual and artistic pursuits including books, games, "collections of curiosities" and pictures on the wall.[85]

Patients were encouraged to take up various crafts such as painting, rug weaving, and carpentry to promote a sense of pride and achievement. In addition, all the patients who could were expected to work—in the kitchen, laundry, print shop, boiler room, gardens, and the farm operation. My mother worked in the employees' kitchen, an obvious choice given her background in the restaurant business. Pearl rather superciliously referred to Gretchen's social life that included playing cards and dancing: "am afraid that's about her natural caliber."

The institute was practically self-sufficient with even its own fire department. The farm was a fully functional operation with at one time over six hundred acres in production of hay, oats, potatoes, vegetables, and sweet corn in addition to raising hogs and milk cows.[86] The 1950 employee handbook is very direct about its expectations of how patients were to be treated.

> 1. Every patient is a person and is to be treated as such; patients are to be shown the respect due any human being. 2. Address all patients by their proper names, using Mr., Mrs. or Miss unless the patient requests you to address him otherwise ... 11. Restraints as such are obsolete in this institution, in case of emergency, where the patient may harm himself, a surgical restraint or wristlet may be applied temporarily only with a written order from the physician in charge ... 15. Never ask a patient to perform any task you would not do yourself. Always work with your patients—never order—ask.[87]

Independence, however, was of course not idyllic. Like the rest of the psychiatric world, the staff there was limited in the treatments available for them to administer. Between 1950 and sometime in 1952, 145 transorbital lobotomies were performed there.[88] And as wonderful as the handbook sounds, patients were of course restricted in their movements and their mail was censored.

When I visited Independence, which has a much reduced population, the person who gave me a tour of the facility was a former attendant who had worked there for many years though after my mother's time. His obviously sincere compassion for the often difficult patients he cared for and his message to school groups that mental illness is an illness like any other and that the mentally ill should not be shunned is a testament to the continuity of the caring culture that was at the heart of the Kirkbride system.

The superintendent of the institute when my mother was there was Max E. Witte (pronounced *witty*). He felt from the beginning that my mother would be able to leave the Institute. "This girl is making a good adjustment." He had an optimism obviously not shared by the rest of my family.

Witte's major aim was getting my mother to the point where she could be released and united with her husband and children, so he kept arranging for visits home with her mother. Since my mother was not a resident of Iowa, there hung over the whole situation the question of whether she could remain at the Institute or not. Adverse to expressing his real feelings, my father never told Witte directly that he did not want my mother back; he kept silent on that issue and did not visit or write my mother once. That alone spoke volumes, but Witte still kept coming up with possibilities for my mother and father to see each other and reestablish their relationship.

At the beginning of March 1951, Witte sent a letter to my father requesting permission to sterilize my mother. However, he believed that her sex drive was probably part of her readjustment to her transorbital lobotomy and that it would most likely disappear in time. Nana was all for the operation, and Pearl also begin to feel "anxious for it." "If she *should get promiscuous* with possible effects and there were no divorce Everett would be responsible for the care of an illegitimate child that might result" (italics mine). But there is no evidence she had been promiscuous. Again, those around my mother were afraid of what she might do, not what she actually did. Sex seems to have been the entire focus of their concerns; there is no mention of paranoia or persecutory notions.

The thought of sterilization is of course shocking. Laws making the practice legal in mental institutions were passed in a number of states in the early twentieth century, including Iowa,[89] and continued well into the early 1960s.[90] They were part of the eugenics movement whose aim was to "improve" the genetic makeup of the population. The belief was that mental illness could be inherited, so if mental patients were sterilized, mental illness would decrease in the population at large.

But I do not think eugenics was the reason for Witte's suggestion. My mother already had two children and was older. I think he wanted to close off the possibility of my mother's conceiving so her family would be comfortable with her being released from institutionalization, if it turned out she could not, as a non-resident of Iowa, remain at Independence. That question dragged on for most of 1951.

Sterilization certainly would have addressed my father's earlier concerns about living together as man and wife, but that was not what he wanted; he wanted my mother out of his life. My father consulted his lawyer and Freeman before saying no to Witte. Without my father's permission, the sterilization operation never happened.

At the end of March, Witte had my mother go to her mother's home on a trial visit, which apparently went very well. Nana stated in her interview with a staff member,

> The patient got along exceptionally well during her trial visit home. She appeared very normal to things around her. She assisted with the cooking and cleaning. She slept extremely well at night. She arose about 6:30 in the morning because of her pattern [of] development here at the hospital.
>
> She was anxious to see her children, who were in Washington D.C. of course and she was unable to see them, but was allowed to talk to her husband and children over the telephone. She was close to her mother during the entire time and showed no abnormal sex tendencies whatever. They visited with some friends and played cards on several occasions and attended an entertainment.

When my mother telephoned us, I answered the phone and talked to her, then my father talked "carefully" as Pearl put it. Finally, my father and I each talked to Nana. I remember nothing specific about the phone call except that I was glad to talk to her. Otherwise, Ricky and I received occasional letters from her. I remember her putting drawings of cartoon characters on a letter to me.

But a comment by Nana in her report upon returning my mother to Independence reveals some tension in her relationship with my father.

> The only remarks that she [Gretchen] made that she should not was that she did not think she would be happy with her husband again. The informant [Nana] now thinks that he possibly is not the best type of individual to be around her. She has reached this conclusion because of his recent attitude toward her. He has shown little interest in the patient. Does not seem to find time to come and see her or write to her. The mother would be willing to take the patient to her home in Dubuque or if we thought it wise to obtain a position elsewhere, she would agree to that also. She will allow the hospital to make the necessary recommendations in regard to the patient's future.

Again, Nana was the one who was assuming the responsibility and taking the action, not my father. He was an expert in passive resistance.

From comments in Pearl's letters to Christine and Louis, it became clear that there was a change in the collaboration between my father and Nana. With my mother on her hands, Nana kept delaying her return to Hyattsville to look after us and relieve Pearl. Then with the doctor's talk of Gretchen's improving, Nana wrote that if Gretchen were released, Witte thought it would be best if she worked outside the home so she "couldn't 'brood.'" That meant no more suburban housewife, which "burned up" Pearl, who thought that was a married woman's duty.

Nana would then take care of us and the house in Hyattsville, but my father was opposed to any such arrangement, and Pearl reported his saying he

> would positively not live with her [Gretchen] again and be the "goat" in an impossible situation. It would be about the only way for Mrs. R to stay in D. and work out the situation with the hospital there and supervise Gretchen's activities under the doctor's [*sic*] there for the summer anyway.

Pearl reported that Nana had written a letter to Everett

> wondering what she did that Everett didn't write. She said the Drs. said Gretchen would "get well" and said her place was there now, etc. as tho' [*sic*] we hadn't said all the time that she should stay and we were getting along well. I have written oftener to tell of what we were doing, so he likely felt there wasn't much for him to write about. He gets pretty worn. He wrote her a letter Tues. nite [*sic*] telling her that it was the thing for her to stay there and he planned to have his children and his parents here to bring things to a focus. Wrote quite a letter. Hope reaction will be good.

The reaction was good. Nana praised my father for "being so good to G. along. That she [Nana] would come to W. sometime during the summer. Said Gr. was better but the Dr. said it would take a long time."

Meanwhile, efforts continued to get my father to Independence. Pearl mentioned that he got a letter from Gretchen "which was quite causal and suggested he 'arrange his business' to come and talk over plans for the children etc. Which of course is as futile as ever."

As patients' mail was screened at Independence, Witte may have asked my mother to write the letter to see what my father's reaction would be. Predictably, my father did not go. Witte also wrote my father at the end of March asking him to come to Independence and see how Gretchen "reacts" to him. As Pearl put it, "He [Everett] doesn't want *any* reaction and is firm on that point. He will not live with her." He did not, however, tell that directly to Witte but instead, at Witte's request, sent him a

> "case history" similar to the one Dr. Freeman has. [Unfortunately, neither letter was in the patient files of Freeman or Independence.] He doesn't feel it expedient to go to Ind. and have an interview to see how she [Gretchen] would "react" and of course time and expense is important, and nothing gained. She would act whatever part she wanted to play anyway.

Again, the idea surfaced that my mother would somehow hide her true self.

My father definitely wanted the ball in Nana's court. So did Pearl, who began to urge Christine and Louis to come to Hyattsville for the summer to "help hold the line unless G were transferred to Maryland instead of released. Even then Mrs. R has her apt. [in Dubuque] and could wait until our 'term was up.'" In other words, we the Rebs, in full force, would get to hold onto the children. "Everett isn't anxious to have her [Gretchen's] supervision too much either. He says if they both come back here he will get a room near his office or another job but that would be hard to really do." This was an infantile reaction and again a withdrawal from any direct confrontation of the issues.

The extended summer family vacation was just part of Pearl's campaign to have Christine along with Louis come to Hyattsville to take care of Ricky and me. From the start, her letters stress how wearing the care of us was.

> I really am not able nor quite capable of taking over entirely, care and discipline and planning clothes, etc. even with Everett being as good as he is, but he is gone so much and the children are quite wearing for all the time and various characteristics. You would be "good medicine" for Robbie.

I am sure I sensed Pearl's weariness and lack of enthusiasm for her role. All this just fed my earlier belief that I was "too much" for those around me and that I was more an imposition than a desired member of the family. That feeling never went away and would crop up throughout my life. I also sensed the uncertainty and tension that existed about Ricky's and my situation. It made me wary about what was going to happen next and reinforced my desire to be independent. It was hard to live in the moment if you could not count on any surety.

Chapter 16

Rebellion in Hyattsville and Independence

With Pearl as my caretaker, I was trying hard to be independent and keep myself intact in the only way I knew how—by strenuous opposition. That may at first sound contradictory to what I just said about feeling that I was "too much." But actually, that feeling fed into my desire for independence; if others could not cope with me, I had to cope for myself. I refused to let Pearl comb my hair, and I would strew toilet paper all over as I rushed from the bathroom to get outside.

My strenuous opposition brought a strenuous reaction. Pearl and my father viewed me as being like my mother not only in my "willfulness and contrariness" but also in my sexual preoccupation with masturbation and trying to remain a Catholic. Masturbation for me was just a way of giving myself pleasure. I even thought of a good side to it as it stopped the need for peeing, and I thought that might come in handy.

The campaign to change me was pressed hard. Pearl even thought I should have a clitorectomy. On March 6, 1951, Pearl wrote to Christine and Louis,

> Robbie shows signs of being much more pleasant, and we feel quite encouraged. The firm stands, and even slaps sort of brot [*sic*] her to mind a bit and I talked some plain facts to her, which she resented but it soaked in some. She has the nervous tension of masturbating at times, which I believe is connected with her willfulness and really hatefulness. One's heart aches for her but it is better to seem a little harsh than to pamper her, which didn't work anyway. I told Everett I think she should have that slight operation of snipping a part, can't remember that name, but is done in such cases and similar to circumcision in boys and he is going to consult the doctor.

Even when I tried to reach out, no one apparently believed I was sincere about that. I commented on how delicious Pearl's strawberry shortcake was, and Pearl in turn commented to Christine, "She was cultivating her 'altruism,' but made us feel like a silver lining. She has been positively rude and unkind. I sit by or read a story while she goes to sleep, but she sleeps alone now." I was very scared to go to sleep and wanted someone by my side.

A few days later, more complaints about me and then a withdrawal of affection.

I am not counting much on real enjoyment with Robbie's fixation of wilfilness [*sic*] and self-centeredness. I'm afraid it is ingrained and the environment has aggravated it. In fact I fear for her future. Everett has to scold and even threaten to get her to react in any way excepting contrariness so we both have adopted a rather unfeeling way. She has been cajoled and pampered so that doesn't have any effect. I've slapped her twice which really gave her some pause and believe a little more adult approach will be a possible help and I plan to talk it over with Mrs. R. when I see her again. I remember Gretchen told that she hardly "wiped her own nose" before she was 7, and hope Mrs. R will see that being too helpful and overseeing is a detriment ... She just asked me to come and sit (and not talk!) while she goes to sleep. She doesn't cough anymore. I sometimes read her a story or two (at <u>my</u> risk!) but Everett said none tonite [*sic*] ... I'm not sorry I came but having to deal constantly with a "problem child" that one had no part in training and really a stranger is difficult.

I call this photograph "The Grey Eminence."

When Easter came, I asserted myself more and asked to go to "my church." So my father took me to the local Catholic church for 9:00 a.m. Mass and came back for me at 10:00 a.m. I was up front near the altar, so he could not get my attention at that time. When Mass was over, I went out to the parking lot looking for him. Soon, the whole place was deserted, and my father was still not there. Perhaps it had been deliberate—to teach me a lesson. I became nervous and scared, so I decided to walk home. I do not know how far it was, but I was at home when everyone came back from looking for me. That of course caused a great uproar. I still, however, continued to attend Mass. I suspect my father allowed that to avoid a confrontation with my mother over the issue.

I do not have her letter to her mother, but Christine obviously reacted sharply to Pearl's talk of slapping me. Pearl responded,

> I was rather surprised and pained at the way you took what I'd said about Robbie. I meant to explain how placating and trying to get along seemed to make her stubborn and rude and the slaps, which weren't painful, seemed to sort of "shock" her into a different frame of mind and she has been doing better. Something like a dash of cold water for tantrums or convulsions. I take her part with Ricky when there is occasion and even look for the chance. I do fear she has inherited that willfulness and contrariness from G. as well as sex disturbance so feel it important to see the pattern changed before it gets set. She will cross her legs up in front and work herself up and down on the davenport or chair. I told her not to, it made her nervous and she said she would if she wanted to and looked mad. Think that brot [sic] one slap. She was better for awhile [sic] but last nite [sic] and tonight she did that way.

At this time, I had lingering bronchitis; the doctor came to give me a penicillin shot (doctors made house calls in those days). Apparently, I had a vaginal condition of some sort, and the doctor thought I should see a gynecologist. I have vivid memories of the examination and thought it humiliating. It turned out that the condition was due to my masturbating.

The doctor told me that if I did not stop, they would have to "cut it off." I of course had no idea he was talking about my clitoris; I did not know what a clitoris was. I thought he was referring to one of my legs, and though I was fearful at first, I came to think of it as ridiculous and not likely to happen. So I continued to masturbate but more covertly. The gynecologist recommended that I see a psychiatrist. Pearl reported that Everett might consult Freeman

> as he knows the background … but I have not seen her do the contortions, since Everett spoke real abruptly to her about stopping. She seems to need stiff rebuke to penetrate or give her a standard. One wonders because different traits follow too much the pattern of Gretchen's.

Freeman had performed lobotomies on children as young as four.[91] I was just seven.

Even when I had normal little girl concerns, I received no sympathy.

> Robbie was "low" because her hair isn't curly and other girls at school are prettier, etc. It doesn't do any good to try to build up her morale. Everett says she is just like Gretchen that way and he gets tired coping with it but of course is pretty much ups and down to all but some adapt themselves better and are less self-centered.

Maybe someone could have said he or she loved me just the way I looked. I obviously needed discipline, but I also needed to be cared for and about. Pearl made sure I was dressed and fed and went on educational outings, but she did not love me. Being "fond" of me, as she mentioned once, was not the same as loving me.

Pearl's treatment of me contrasted markedly with her treatment of my brother. For that I am grateful. She took to him immediately. In the same letter in which she first complained about my behavior, she stated, "Rickie is quite a satisfaction." And Ricky became quite attached to her. He was very attentive to her when she was not feeling well, and when she put on the same gray coat and hat she had worn when she arrived, Ricky "looked distressed and said 'Where you goin'? don't want you to go' so I told him we were all going in the car and he seemed quite relieved."

She did have to scold him occasionally, but that was because he would get into things he shouldn't. She even shortened for Ricky the little prayer we both said at bedtime: "Now I lay me down to sleep." She left out the last part: "If I should die before I wake, I pray the Lord my soul to take." That part always scared me, but Pearl did not modify the nightly prayer for me.

Pearl and Ricks on an excursion to the Capitol

As my "self-centeredness" and masturbation were being dealt with, my grandmother began a campaign to pry me from Catholicism. While I was sick in bed with bronchitis, she sat with me listening on the radio to famous Methodist preachers at the time such as Dr. Norman Vincent Peale. She wrote to Christine that I asked Pearl

> if Dr. P was a Catholic and tho't [*sic*] he was likely a priest anyway, and I said no, they all make good talks and told her afterwards he is a Methodist and that her Daddy belonged to that church. She said "I know." She is quite a person, difficult but one is fond of her and anxious to be understood.

I slowly and rather tentatively began to go to Methodist services with the rest of the family. In early April, Pearl reported that we all attended church services together

> and got along nicely excepting Ricky got restless the last half hour. It was rather prolonged … Roberta was O.K. and joined in parts of it with Everett's book. She said afterwards it was long, and he remarked how long she stays at the Catholic services, but I was glad we got to go all together once.

I am sure that I wanted to be accepted, and this was an important reason for my attending Methodist services with little protest. But my defection as it were from the Catholic Church was largely due to my reaction to a priest during confession. Trying to be scrupulously honest, at the end of my confession, I said that I had told him all the sins I could think of. The priest was rather harsh and rebuked me about that; he said I should try harder. He must have thought I was being evasive. I decided that his reaction was wrong. He should have understood I was doing my best. I never went to confession again and thus stopped going to Mass at the Catholic church. But even in October, Pearl wrote that I was not as "appreciative" of listening to a sermon on the radio as Ricky as I still had "the bias of feeling different, but she does quite well at church keeping track of the songs and readings."

Once Ricky and I discovered Sunday school, however, we became "enthusiastic" about attending. So Everett and Pearl, who had been taking me to the eleven o'clock service with

Ricky in the nursery, went to an earlier service, so Sunday school became part of our routine.

During that time, I was attending Greenbelt Elementary School, where I had no friends in my class, but I was a good reader and was in the highest reading group. That was good for my self-esteem. Relying on academic performance for self-esteem to the degree that I did was, however, in the end not healthy. Much later, as I entered graduate school, I panicked at major points particularly just before my orals, curling up into a fetal position on the floor, and in the end, I withdrew from the program rather than risk possibly failing.

Back at Independence, Nana had my mother for another leave in May. Family letters reveal at this time that my mother had formed a romantic relationship with a female patient at the Institute. I can imagine that my mother found solace in this relationship, which met her need for love. But she was certainly in a psychotic state. "Gretchen refused to do anything and smoked constantly. She [Gretchen] feels that she is the cause of the present war [Korean War] and that her mother is having sex relations with her husband." She asked her mother to have sexual relations with her too. She was extremely religious and "hears the voice of God. An example of which is 'Hear the rain on the roof, it sounds like the red, white and blue. God is telling me to get a divorce.'"

Nana thought she had visions and hallucinations because Gretchen would continually look up and speak of seeing two crosses. She "threatened suicide by jumping off a high bridge and stated several times that she did not want to live without her husband." My mother was obviously still worse off after the lobotomy than before.

A report from Independence stated,

> The mother feels that the major cause of the patient's illness is because the patient married outside of the church and this has led to the complex dealing with sex. She is unable to explain this further. She feels that Gretchen is just too much for her at this time and that she has her sister [Martha] in the home and that she must take care of Gretchen's children, who are living with Mr. Reb in Washington, D.C. The mother stated that if Mr. Reb does not pay for hospitalization that she will.

Meanwhile in Hyattsville, I was improving somewhat in Pearl's and my father's eyes. I still was

> quite headless and touchy, but has a more agreeable manner and minds much better. Can comb her hair now ... Roberta seems to be real fine in nearly all ways. Of course has some wilful [*sic*], careless ways, but not extreme now and hasn't done that nervous squeezing, so he [Everett] may not consult Dr. Freeman and make a "case" of her as long as she is improving all around.

Thank goodness for that. But I was never in her eyes going to escape criticism. On a weekend in May, Pearl described my helping out with all the kids about the house by "chaperoning" them. "She is getting 'sweeter' all the time but lacks mostly in neatness and pitching her voice and rushing in and out of things, but is so much more dependable." That seemed more like the expectations of a young adult and not someone who was just seven. Pearl was truly devoid of empathy.

My father and Pearl did, however, start taking an interest in the more positive things I did. "Ricky and I went with Everett to the school Health program. He took the time off to encourage her interest and it was real good. She had quite a part in one skit and looked right nice in her yellow dress and hair ribbons." As Pearl stated, I "was being nicer mostly."

Meanwhile, according to Pearl, Witte wrote my father and "indicated he tho't [*sic*] later she [Gretchen] might be able to resume the 'marital status' which is something Everett is firm against. There is no real affection on either side now to build on and E. will oppose it."

Pearl was nervous about a letter she had received from Nana indicating that she expected Gretchen to remain at Independence until she was "cured" and giving the impression that she

> wants to count on being here part of the time and Everett doesn't want it to work out that way so I feel some nervous as to meeting it all. She spoke before of coming at Robbie's birthday which would be all right, unless it would upset what we've gained in control, adjustments, of course she would want to see them.

The plan they worked out, however, avoided Nana's coming to Hyattsville for my birthday. It involved Ricky and me going to Christine's house in Chicago with Pearl and Louis after the planned summer trip and for Nana to

> get them there for 2, 3 or 4 weeks visit in Dubuque for her [my] birthday Aug. 17th. Hope that will take care of that part. Everett would have that month or little over to finish up the house and furnishings and plan for the fall time.

As mentioned, my mother apparently had not done well on her last home visit.

> Will write a little this morning to let you know the latest we heard from Mrs. R. She says Gretchen isn't doing well there and wants to [go] back to hospital and cries for a woman there. Said she Gretchen didn't want to see the children so for us not to send them (which will simplify plans but hard to contemplate). Mrs. R said she was going to Minnesota "to get away from it all" for awhile [sic] and then come to W. for a visit. She is "heartbroken" she says, and is going to write Dr. Witte the circumstances. Said she hadn't thot [sic] G. was able to leave hospital, but they wanted to try it out. She [Gretchen] had written and said over phone that she was "wonderful" but I tho't [sic] she might not react very well when it came to the test. Hope G. will be retained there at Iowa

instead of being transferred here, as she seems to be enjoying it there and after all her mother could oversee her some.

Nana took Gretchen back to the hospital, but as Pearl reported,

> The Dr. wanted her to stay out awhile [*sic*] at least, and she wrote as tho [*sic*] things were good, but the last 2 letters told of her being off again and back to Ind. Then the last one told of her [Gretchen] running off from the hospital because she could not be with the women she was too fond of (probably homosexual). All very sad and difficult. Everett is paying around $65 a month [about $650 in today's money] for her care there and that would be the best way to do.

Since the Independence Mental Health Institute sat in the midst of miles of farmland, it was difficult for patients who ran away to get far. There are no details available about my mother's attempt, but she was obviously brought back to the Institute unharmed. Pearl's letter also indicated that the decision about whether my mother could stay on at the Institute had not yet been made. Witte was still trying his best to have her released and reunited with my father.

When my mother was interviewed by Witte after she was brought back to Independence, it was clear that Nana was right and that my mother was not really ready to be outside the institution. My mother told Witte,

Here before she went home there were a lot of suggestions and she would see people here who reminded her of individuals she had known in the past. She was worried about some dreams that she is not proud of [so she was feeling the burden of guilt]. She was worried about people said that she might be sterilized because of masturbation [so she somehow knew of the plans, although her masturbation was not the issue but her potential promiscuity].

At that time, she revealed more about her masturbatory activities.

There was masturbation on a few occasions when she was sick at 14 or 15. When 17 there was some mutual masturbation in Chicago at 19 or 20, then again was some masturbation and also when she was pregnant with daughter.

When at home, there was a lot of propaganda that she didn't know what complete union was and that they were trying to keep her in Dubuque away from her husband. People seemed to be reading her mind. Different suggestions were made.

I can find no reference to "complete union" in Catholic doctrine on marriage. I can only speculate that it relates to her not having been married in the church.

Says starting in Washington and coming clear out here, there has been a lot of talk about her having had an illegitimate child, which she never had.

Here, the basis would seem to be the fact that I was listed as "bastard" on the register at the time of my baptism.

Patient says before her lobotomy she realized her marriage wasn't going right because her husband was indifferent and didn't take responsibility around the home. After the lobotomy, the patient felt sure that her husband had had relations with other men and women.

That belief seemed to have its basis in my father's not having sex with her and therefore must have been having it elsewhere.

Patient tells of an incident in Washington when the manager of a store was very friendly towards her and asked her to come into his office so he could love her up. After that, she would take the children with her when she entered this store. She had a dream about this man which involved masturbation.

The man's advances, assuming they actually existed, must have sexually aroused her.

After returning from her attempt to run away, she was no longer allowed to work in the employees' cafeteria and was confined to a closed or locked ward where there was someone supervising patients twenty-four hours a day.

In Hyattsville, school was out, and Christine came to join us on several summer excursions. One was to Philadelphia, where I remember seeing the Liberty Bell. The following week, we went to Williamsburg, which I recall as being impressively quaint, like another world. And finally, we went to Ocean City, Maryland, where we walked along the wide boardwalk by the Atlantic Ocean and played the 5¢ slot machines. These were good memories; with Christine present, life seemed calmer and more secure.

In August, my father talked with Freeman, who "still recommended another lobotomy to check further deterioration but doesn't guarantee it. He doesn't think she is in a very good condition, and considers this step necessary." Freeman's records show that he subsequently visited my mother in person. In his autobiography, Freeman listed Independence, Iowa, as one of the places he visited in 1951,[92] and his file on her contains a photograph of her looking rather haggard taken at the time of the visit.

My mother photographed by Freeman in August 1951

Though there is nothing in the patient records at Independence that mentions Freeman's presence, according to family correspondence, he and Witte apparently had a meeting. It would have been interesting to know what these two men had to say to each other. Witte had his own ideas about my mother's situation and was obviously not cowed by Freeman's reputation.

According to Pearl, Freeman reported to my father that

> the second lobotomy would be done at Ind. and that Dr. Witte thinks it can be arranged for her to stay on there (as we hoped). Ev asked if he tho't [sic] she ever could take up a mother's part and he [Freeman] doubted it. He [Everett] wrote to Dr. W. for a report from the conference and will write to Mrs. R. who thinks there should be no tho't [sic] of her being released home, or with her so trust something permanent can be planned and she feel as settled as possible. Her mother wrote she seemed better and was playing baseball and enjoying herself different ways. That seems the best possible.

But the letter my father got from Witte did not at all concur with Freeman. Witte was in

> favor of transfer to Maryland, so he [Everett] could take her out in the car weekends!! He surely hasn't grasped the situation much. He thinks it is a failure to release her to her mother. He said Dr. F. didn't mention operation [a second lobotomy] so things just hang.

In another letter, Witte straightforwardly stated that Gretchen would need custodial care for quite a while. At the same time, Pearl received a letter from Nana: "She said G. was taking 'shock treatments' again. She had Gretchen out for two days and had had a picnic but she said she wasn't going to take her out again until she was well so you can see just what a daze things are in."

Meanwhile in late July, my mother had another short leave home with Ricky and me there. It was the first time we had seen her since December. Nana reported to the Institute that

> she seemed to get along well, taking care of her children and doing more house work than usual. Thursday evening, however, she saw the movie "Show Boat" following which she became upset and confused. She said that she was reminded of her husband and for the first time let out her feelings of resentment and bitterness against him, showing some "fight." Since Thursday night she has been much better.

What that report did not say was that I was with my mother at the movie. *Show Boat* involves several ill-fated love stories including one in which a husband deserted his wife. Seeing *Show Boat* agitated her, and she started to cry. I was upset too and afraid of being sucked into her world.

Not long after that, she disappeared from my life, that is, went back to the Institute. She had asked her mother for a razor blade to take back to the hospital. Nana stated "that she never dared to let her swim alone, and feels very fortunate to have been able to get her back to the hospital."

My father came to get Ricky and me. He and Nana spent a great deal of time in the house discussing matters while I was outside roller skating alone on the sidewalk. I fell and used that as an occasion to cry to get them to pay attention to me.

Shortly after that, my father took us back to Christine's house in Chicago. I will always remember sitting backward in the back seat of the car looking out the window as my grandmother's apartment building faded from view and realizing at that moment that I had lost my mother.

Chapter 17

The Situation Drags On

Ricky and I spent several weeks in Riverdale, Illinois, at Christine's house, which she had purchased for herself and her aging parents. My father apparently returned to Hyattsville to finish the work on the upstairs. I slept on a cot next to Christine's bed. She was a five-ten, large-boned woman. Her physical presence was so comforting to me.

I made a few friends among kids in the neighborhood, and we smoked cattails in the alley. I was sent for swimming lessons at a local park. I was lonely and terrified about this new place as I knew no one there. Christine made special arrangements for me to take a floating device, which in the end I did not use to the obvious annoyance of the teacher. I was humiliated when after taking a shower before going into the pool, I was sent back because I had dirt ingrained in my feet. Strange as it may sound, no one had taught me to pay attention to such things.

During the short time I attended the swimming class, I learned to do the jellyfish float and the dead man's float, which

I thought were good to know in case I ever fell overboard someday.

It is not clear from the medical records whether my mother went on another leave in late July, but there are notes from an interview with her on August 5.

> Says when she was home, she had one discussion with her mother about why she was here and mother was very evasive. Patient says there has been a lot of propaganda and implications that she had a baby by somebody else rather than her husband. Her husband was sterile. She has ignored this because her conscience is clean. She admits she is slightly neurotic because she didn't get love and attention from her husband. She is gifted with a keen sense of imagination ... Patient is quiet more so than would be expected. Hesitates before answer[ing] questions and still shows evidence of guilt.

In the fall of 1951, I was eight and attending yet another school, Bladensburg Elementary. Again, I knew no one there and did not really develop any friendships. I was probably seen as odd as I masturbated a couple of times at my desk in the classroom although no one, not even the teacher, said anything.

I muffed my chance to help the teacher by spilling water on some papers on her desk; for that, I had to stand in the corner. Another time when filling out attendance records; I didn't know how to get the pages out of the notebook, so I tore them out to the teacher's ire.

On Valentine's Day, I got very few valentines. But I could still be assertive. A fat bully in our class tried to break in front of me in line; I wouldn't let him, so he and I got into a quarrel. Instead of siding with me, the teacher reprimanded me and let him get in front. I was mad at the injustice but glad I had stood up for myself. Pearl kept reporting to Christine that I was doing well and seemed happy with school, but I really wasn't and felt very alone.

At Independence, matters remained much up in the air. My father still had not heard from Witte whether my mother could

> be maintained at Ind. hospital. Mrs. R feels every attempt to associate is a failure and says "never again." Although she has felt differently. It is hard for everyone—sort of a continuous drag on sensibilities and consciousness and no workable situation—only endurance.

Christine had asked about writing to Gretchen, whom Christine had always liked, but Pearl responded, "None of us likes to seem 'hard-boiled' when our hearts ache most of the time but trying to meet the situation usually has failed so it seems any sort of correspondence would make things more complex."

At Independence, my mother was getting shock treatments, which Freeman did not think would be of any permanent benefit. Nana wanted another lobotomy as "a final effort." Pearl reported, "As Everett says it begins to seem as if just planning to make a mental patient as comfortable and satisfied as possible might be better than all the treatments."

My mother wrote my father a letter in late September.

> She writes quite brisk about her times and therapies, etc. She takes art and sent a sketch she had made. That's what makes it hard to know she wouldn't stand up at home. This schedule seems to include the things she enjoys without personal responsibility and if so maintained, would be better for her than release to her mother or home surroundings.

In the same letter to Christine, Pearl wrote, probably based on a letter from Nana, that "as far as religion is concerned G. seems to feel she had *it*. She told her mother she didn't need her ... She had God."

At the beginning of October, Pearl got a letter from Nana.

> She said the shock treatments had helped (but Dr. Fr. has told Everett they are not likely to be permanent help). I told you before that G. had written E. again. Quite a jaunty type. She helps in Mrs. Witte's apt. and is in the "open ward" again. No doubt she is better off than released anywhere but what steps they will take remains to be seen. Mrs. R. asked before to have her things and some of Gretchen's sent and Everett boxed up practically everything including her short fur coat.

Helping in Dr. and Mrs. Witte's apartment would have been a very significant privilege marking my mother as very trustworthy. The apartment for the superintendent at Independence is extraordinarily spacious and elegant, with even a little conservatory. It is right at the center of the Institute, just a climb up the grand staircase, which is fit for a mansion, from the reception area.

Nana continued to report to Pearl that Gretchen was doing well at the Institute and

> Dr. W said "if it would just hold," but I don't think he and I know Mrs. R. [Nana] doesn't think she will ever be responsible or right. We are all hopeing she will be able to stay on there. It is almost like going to a boarding school for her.

Finally, there was a resolution to the question.

> Mrs. R said Dr. W has said G. could stay on there with Everett paying the costs, average $68 or $70 per mo. so far [about $700 in today's money]. He recommends an operation but said it wasn't serious in writing to E. Mrs. R said in her letter ... that the doctor tho't [sic] there might be a small tumor or abscess.

That suggestion indicates that the exact nature of my mother's mental illness was puzzling. In fact, to my knowledge, there was never any definitive diagnosis. She was certainly, however, not schizophrenic as Freeman had initially thought. My father signed the consent papers.

The letters from Pearl to Christine and Louis stopped in late November as both had come to live permanently with us in Hyattsville, so I do not know if my mother was operated on for a tumor. There is nothing in the patient files to indicate that occurred, and no one in my family ever mentioned it. I do know that my mother went out on another trial visit over the Christmas holiday to be with her mother. Nana wrote a note to the superintendent when she brought my mother back.

> I did want to talk to you Wednesday when I brought Gretchen back but she wanted to go in with me and so decided I'd write you instead. Gretchen is better, but still not normal. The last day here she started talking about sex, said it was none of my business about her sex life, or with whom she had it. I said nothing as I thought I would not get her back. Several times she was confused about other things.

Chapter 18

Christine Comes to Hyattsville

I turned nine in 1952, a year that was a continuation of the seemingly endless, tumultuous years. What helped make it bearable for me was the presence of my aunt Christine. All along, Pearl had been urging Christine to come and help raise my brother and me. That was in many ways giving up a lot for Pearl. Just a few years previously, her dream of living again with Christine had come true. Borrowing from her life insurance policy for the down payment, Christine had purchased a small, two-bedroom ranch house in a south suburb of Chicago, and her parents moved there from Kansas.

At the time, Christine was a librarian at the Art Institute of Chicago but was contemplating leaving the position. Pearl and my father tried hard to find a suitable position in Washington for her, without success.

In the end, Christine just came with my grandfather Louis. I am sure many factors influenced her decision. First, it was clear that Nana would not be returning to look after us. Second, her mother's health with the stress and strain of dealing with Ricky and me must have worried her. Pearl wrote constantly about needing Christine to talk to and about her ailments, particularly her leg sores. As a consequence, Christine must have decided her presence was necessary.

Christine was an anchor for me. While Pearl was rigid and self-righteous, Christine was calm, flexible, and understanding. She listened, a skill a reference librarian must have to be a good one, and she responded accordingly. She was someone to whom I could talk without fear of being judged. Just her physical presence was calming; she had none of her mother's high-strung nervousness. I loved sitting with her in our armchair physically touching and reading books out loud. I particularly remember *Mistress Marcham's Repose* by T. H. White about an orphan girl who found a group of Lilliputians (from Jonathan Swift's *Gulliver's Travels*). It was laugh-out-loud funny, and we so enjoyed it.

How Christine became who she was and what she did is an amazing story. She was born in 1914 on her parents' farm near Frankfort, Kansas, from whose small high school she graduated in 1930. As my father later related, "Thank God, mother had the gumption to move us to Baldwin so that Christine and I could live at home while going to college. Otherwise, we couldn't afford it."

In Baldwin, Christine worked in the Baker College library to earn money toward tuition. That experience convinced her to become a librarian. Upon graduation with a BA in 1934, she briefly took a teaching job at a small high school but was rescued from that unhappy situation by the offer of the position of assistant librarian at Baker.

She was fortunate for the mentorship she received; in 1937 she was encouraged to take a leave of absence to attend library school at the University of Illinois at Urbana-Champaign, where she received a BS in library science with high honors in 1938 and an MA in 1941.

I am amazed that during this time, she coped well with her mother, who wanted to know everything about her life and continually wished to visit or have Christine come home for a visit. Christine somehow was able to pursue her career path without unduly upsetting her mother, to whom she was grateful for the opportunity to attend college.

In 1941, she returned to Baldwin as head librarian at Baker, but when World War II broke out, she took a leave of absence to join the Army Hostess and Librarian Service. She became post librarian at Winter General Hospital in Topeka, Kansas, just a few weeks before it admitted hundreds of soldiers who had been wounded in North Africa.

After the war, she did not return to Baker. Instead, another of her mentors, a former teacher at the University of Illinois, had become head reference librarian at the University of Chicago, and she offered Christine the assistant position in 1946. That was Christine's dream job, but it did not last long. Pearl had health issues; exactly how they were more severe than usual I do not know, but Christine was persuaded to leave the University of Chicago and return to Baldwin to be with her mother. But she did not sit by her mother's side. She spent as she said "an unhappy 6 months" as assistant librarian at Topeka Public Library and then took off again in 1947 as she accepted the assistant librarian position at the Art

Institute of Chicago's library. It was from that position that she resigned to come to Hyattsville.

Christine at Winter General Hospital

I was looking for strong female role models (not Pearl) at the time, and Christine along with my grandmother Nana and the wife of my father's best friend served me well. I also was a fan of Tugboat Annie, a character in stories run in the *Saturday Evening Post*, who was captain of her own tugboat and able to hold her own in a male world. Christine and my father encouraged me to be an active tomboy.

When Christine first came to Hyattsville in December 1951, however, her major concern was her mother. She worked to introduce a heart-healthy menu for Pearl. That was hard as one of the delights of Pearl's life was a good meal she made or one at a restaurant. That was a regular part of her reporting in all her letters to Christine, and she wanted to know what Christine ate too.

But her high blood pressure had gotten too far out of hand. On the night of March 14, 1952, Pearl had a fatal heart attack. I remember her sitting on the sofa in the living room moaning with her hands on her heart. I took Ricky with me into another room so we would be away from it. I knew they had called an ambulance, but the strangest thing was that the next morning, no one told Ricky and me that she had died. Christine, Louis, and my father were somber, but I heard no crying or even talking.

They made plans to take her body to Baldwin for burial, but I was left behind probably because of school. I stayed with the next-door neighbors all alone on the top floor. I remember asking the mother of that family to sit by me while I went to sleep, which she kindly did. My family had arranged what they thought was a special treat—someone to take me to see the *Wizard of Oz*. But in fact, the movie scared me as I was afraid of the wicked witch.

Amid all that, later that spring, I was molested by a girlfriend's father. He was a bulky, beer-drinking military man who was often away from home. I went to visit my friend; she wasn't there, but her father was; he was watching television with a beer can by his side. I do not remember if he said for me to come in. I was eager to please adults and for them to like me, so I went in and sat on the floor by his chair. He reached in my pants and began masturbating me. I knew of course about masturbation, and it felt stimulating, but I knew it was wrong for him to do that. I moved away but was afraid he would be upset with me, so I moved back, and he masturbated me again.

I went home and told my father and Christine what had happened. They had a long discussion of which I was not a part. They finally told me I should never go into that house again. No one blamed me, but no one consoled me or talked about it further with me. All I had was the rule, which I punctiliously followed even though my friend and her mother wondered why and the father was not present. I later learned from a gastroenterologist that child sexual abuse is associated with irritable bowel syndrome.

We now know sexual abuse was and is unfortunately not uncommon. And like many sufferers, I have felt guilt over the years about it, that I should have somehow known better and never gone back a second time. But that is harsh judgment on an eight-year-old who was going through what I was going through. I have come to accept that it was not my fault and mentally bash the man over the head with a table lamp. Why a table lamp I don't know—just something handy.

My mother's patient record is blank for the first nine months of 1952. She apparently did not go out on any more trial visits during that time; she seemed to have adapted to the environment at the hospital. Ricky and I went that summer to see Nana, and there was an empty feeling about the whole visit.

Later that summer, my father left me in the care of a family whose father was his best friend and whose mother my father greatly admired. She was a kind-hearted, no-nonsense woman. Her and her husband's relationship became my model of what a good marriage should be like. They had two boys close to my age. I do not know why Christine was not looking after me, but I surmise that she and Louis took Ricky and were settling matters in Chicago about her house.

I had a horrible nightmare that first night there about a giant spider attacking me, and I woke up screaming. The mother came to comfort me, and she persuaded her older son to let me have one of his teddy bears to sleep with. I had turned nine and was certainly beyond teddy bears, but I slept with it the whole time I was there.

I was taken to horseback riding lessons, something I always wanted (along with a horse, which I never got), and I did enjoy that and reading the many Oz books they had. I could put one away in a day.

My father had gone to Beirut, Lebanon for training at the American University of Beirut and to become acquainted with personnel in major cities in the Middle East in preparation for his eventual assignment there. I knew my father was overseas, but I knew nothing about why he was there. I also did not know that at that time, he was transferred to the United States Information Agency (USIA), which had just been established by President Eisenhower to handle public relations overseas. When he came home, he shared a picture of himself wearing a fez and riding a camel, which I thought looked very exotic. In November 1952, as mentioned earlier, he was made chief of the Middle East Bureau of the USIA.

In the fall, my father, Christine, Louis, Ricky, and I were back together as a family. I returned to my original school, Riverdale Elementary, and stayed there for the next three years. That gave some stability to my life and allowed me to make friends (and have girl talk), participate in numerous activities including glee

My father "relaxes" on a camel in Egypt.

club, and take clarinet lessons at school and piano lessons at home. I am not musical and did not much care for the piano, but the piano had been my mother's, and I think my father felt it was her wish that I use it.

Back in Independence, somehow through Witte's efforts, my mother became well enough in October 1952 to be paroled, released conditionally, so that if she showed signs of needing institutionalization again, that could occur without another legal proceeding. I think Witte's patience and belief in her ability to be released played the most important role in her recovery. Expectations are powerful motivators. Almost immediately, she got a job as a sales clerk in a department store. Freeman was later to claim her as one of his successes, but she was not his success; she was Witte's and his staff's success.

Chapter 19

My Mother in Dubuque

When Ricky and I visited our mother in the summer of 1953, I was turning ten and Ricky was nearing six. We stayed with her in the same apartment we had lived in when Ricky and I were very young; it had hot water then but still no facilities for bathing. Nana, however, had moved into the apartment below and had a shower we used.

I remember being with my mother when she cashed out her cash register and her figures did not match; one of the employees made a snide remark about her having been institutionalized, which infuriated me. I was never embarrassed by my mother's institutionalization.

She also did waitressing at night in a tavern in East Dubuque, Illinois, right across the Mississippi River from Dubuque. East Dubuque was wet while Dubuque was dry. I saw my mother handling the banter with patrons and admired how she wove in and out of the crowd.

It was Christine who told me about the lobotomy though she did not use that word. She explained that an instrument had been stuck up my mother's eye socket and had severed some nerves to make her less emotional. She said that as a result, my mother had lost her "sparkle." I remember surreptitiously trying to see in my mother's eye sockets if there were scars where the operation had taken place. There weren't.

Since at that time I knew nothing of my mother's career in Chicago or what the effects of a lobotomy might be, I simply accepted that she was as I found her. There was nothing unusual or strange about her behavior, but there was no hint of the vivacious, effervescent personality that I later found in her scrapbooks and diary. To ignorant me, she appeared as someone who in the end could not live in a world larger than Dubuque. I never knew she had gone to college or cared much for cultural things.

She only once told the story of flying in an airplane to Racine but in rather vague and general terms. I never knew her to spend any significant time painting. Her apartment remained the same throughout my visits. She made no effort to modernize it or change it in any way, not like the way she had thrown herself into decorating when we first moved to the house in Hyattsville. The drive and imagination had been taken from her.

But my mother was a very kind person. She had a great deal of empathy for others particularly young people, several of whom she took under her wing, perhaps to make up in some small way for the fact that she did not have Ricks and me around much. She taught swimming at the local YMCA to physically challenged youngsters.

My mother was sometimes emotional; she almost burst into tears when I remarked that I did not like housework. She felt that was the way to work out her anxieties. She seemed just a little slower than I remembered as a younger child, and she had very simple interests often centered on religion. We bought bread at a Trappist monastery and visited a religious grotto constructed of shells and ceramic objects embedded in concrete. On Sunday mornings when my mother went to church, I know she hoped I would be awake so she could cajole me into coming, a request I did not feel I could refuse, so I took to pretending I was asleep until she was out the door. She never deliberately woke me up or talked to me about returning to Catholicism.

Freeman followed my mother's condition all her life. He visited her a second time in May 1959 and took another of his pictures documenting his patients. She looked wonderful and was still working. He never visited again, but he did ask for periodic reports and wrote her postcards and

Freeman's photograph of
my mother in 1959

at least one letter my grandmother preserved. I never heard

my mother talk about Freeman or the lobotomy, nor did my father ever mention him or the procedure.

In his patient notes, Freeman indicated "divorce" for August 1953. Maryland court records show that my father filed for divorce in June that year, but the divorce was not finalized until almost two years later. Thus I believe it was in the fall of 1953 that Nana drove my mother to Hyattsville to stay in a nearby motel where us kids could visit.

Then one day for whatever reason, Nana drove her to our house, and I watched as my mother pleaded on the front lawn of our house with outstretched arms and tears running down her cheek for my father to take her back. He was very curt and angry and refused to do so. I felt so sorry for my mother to be humiliated in that way.

My mother never had another episode of mental illness and never returned to the Institute. She was finally certified as "recovered" in October 1954. But there was obviously no possibility of reconciliation with my father by that time. Until I did the research for this book, I did not know when my parents divorced. It turns out it was finalized in February 1955 with my father having complete custody of us children with a vague statement about the custody "being subject to the right of the defendant [my mother] to see them at reasonable times." My father was not generous with the amount of time we saw her.

He told me years later that Nana had driven a hard bargain in terms of the monetary settlement. One could hardly blame her as in effect, my father had abandoned my mother to her. My mother once commented rather bitterly that she could not contest our custody as she had been institutionalized. It must have been a major blow, but she never spoke ill of my father to us kids, nor did my father speak ill of her—except for the supposed marriage-night confession he mentioned long after her death.

My father did impart another of his strange communications a few years later. He told me he had decided to obtain custody because my mother wanted to split Ricky and me up. She wanted to raise me and have Ricky cared for by one of her childless aunts and uncles in Dubuque. I am certainly glad Ricky and I remained together and with my father as he offered the opportunities and excitement of a wider world. But my father made it sound like he was doing us a favor rather than wanting us for ourselves, which I know was not the impression he wanted to give. It was just another instance of his not being aware of how his words and actions affected others.

Chapter 20

A Semblance of Normalcy

Over the following two years, Ricky and I visited our mother and Nana only once a year in the summer, so circumstances made my mother a distant figure in my life. We wrote letters and sent cards on Mother's Day, but that of course did not take the place of physical presence.

Over those years in Hyattsville, Christine, Louis, and my father made a home for Ricky and me. Christine was someone to whom I could talk about things that bothered me such as an unsettling dream I had about Pearl's coming back and not liking the furniture in the living room. She very gently got me to stop masturbating. She taught me many useful

skills such as how to sew using her old treadle machine—if you have seen the cartoon version of *How the Grinch Stole Christmas*, you have seen a treadle machine in action. Later in my life, when money was short, I made a lot of my own clothes and items for my children including sleeping bags and my daughter's prom dress.

But I owe even more to Christine for the intellectual gifts she gave me. She furthered my love of reading. With her as a model, I learned that females did not need to hide being smart, so I continued to do well in school. She told me that in graduate school, she would distill a course down until she would summarize it in one sentence. That idea of focusing on the essentials served me well in life and in my career.

There was a lighter side to her as well. Christine had many joys she shared with me. One was collecting elephants. She kept them in an old steamer trunk, and I delighted in rummaging through it and examining them. She loved the Spanish flamenco dancer José Greco, and she took me to see him several times. I have a pair of castanets I bought in Spain, and I would give my right arm to learn flamenco. She was an avid fan of the comic strip *Pogo* and made me a fan of it too. We would read some of the strips together and laugh.

She was also an avid White Sox fan, and I became one and still am. Later, as head of Reference Services at the University of Chicago, she made sure the library ordered the autobiography of the legendary White Sox owner Bill Veeck, *Veeck as in Wretch*.

Most of all, I remember the values Christine as well as my father instilled in me, which makes his treatment of my mother particularly upsetting. Each believed in the dictum that you were no better than anyone else, that no one was better than you, and that you should treat everyone with respect. When Christine finally took a part-time job at the University of Maryland library, we hired a maid. The woman kept complaining to Christine that she could not make out her handwriting on the notes Christine would leave about what needed to be done. After that happened several times, Christine realized that the woman could not read. She explained that to me and asked me to volunteer to read it aloud to avoid any embarrassment.

Christine and my father also shared their lack of prejudice toward minority groups. I encountered only whites like myself in the neighborhood or school, but they planted in me their attitude about racial injustice. I went on in later years to be involved in the civil rights movement in Chicago. A friend of my father must have been involved in actions opposing segregation as one Sunday we attended a service at an African-American church where the friend was receiving an honor.

In those years, my father also became a more significant part of Ricky's and my lives. Perhaps that was a function of our being older and his mother not being a constant presence. At that time, my father was a disciplinarian but also someone with whom I had fun experiences. Nonetheless, I still had some deep-seated hostility toward him for disrupting my life. One time out of pure spite, I put ice on the seat of his car. When he sat on it, the result was quite a scene. I was not sorry. My punishments for any misbehavior were a spanking (which were few) and going to bed without supper, neither of which I really cared about.

Like Christine, my father was a sports fan. He would practice baseball with us, particularly with Ricky, whom he hoped he could make into a switch hitter, and tennis, which was a sport he had loved since his college days. I played tackle football with the boys in the neighborhood and triumphantly dragged a would-be tackler across the goal line. My father

would take us to ball games, and we watched sports together on TV. He threw himself into celebrating Christmas and Easter.

On Sundays, we went for long drives and sang or were quizzed on spelling—I am a poor speller. We regularly roasted hotdogs on Sunday evenings over the fire in our living room fireplace. My father would go into the nearby woods and cut fresh branches that he would whittle to a point with a knife so we could poke the hotdogs on. We would eat and watch TV together although the amount of TV we were allowed to watch was strictly monitored. We were supposed to be reading books, painting pictures, or running around outside. On weekends, we regularly visited with the families of my father's coworkers, one Jewish and the other Catholic. I played with their children, and it all gave me a family feeling.

We got in many fights in our neighborhood, and I often fought boys. I remember running in the house one time to tell my father about it. I expected him to come and threaten the boy. He was reading the newspaper and told me I could stay in or go out—it was up to me. I got bored with being inside, so I went out and fought.

In short, my father fostered my independence; he often told me I had a good head on my shoulders and I should use it. However, my brother just attributes it to "benign neglect."

Grandpa Louis would plant a garden with us in the difficult clay soil of our backyard and pop "real" popcorn by rubbing dried cobs of corn together to dislodge the kernels and then heat them in an iron skillet.

Summer evenings were hot; we had no fans or air conditioning, and I would get prickly heat rash on the back of my neck. We caught fireflies, knocked Japanese beetles from the bushes in the yard into bottles, collected tadpoles in the pools made by the creek at the bottom of the street, and ate watermelon on the front steps and then had seed-spitting contests. We kids would spin around until we were so dizzy that we fell down and watched the clouds whirl above our heads. We played marbles, hide-and-go-seek, Mother May I, jacks, leapfrog, and hopscotch. I ran barefoot most of the summer; in the fall when I went back to school, my shoes felt awkward and confining.

In the winter, us neighborhood kids would of course have snowball fights from behind our respective snow forts, and we made snowmen. The only available clothing for winter in those days was heavy wool pants and tops and rubber boots. I would stay outside until my hands and feet were numb. When I came in, Christine would put my feet in the bathtub and run warm water over them until the feeling came back. Then she would fix hot chocolate with a marshmallow melting in it.

Chapter 21

Off to Beirut

After several years of relative normalcy in our lives, Ricky and I were again uprooted emotionally and physically in 1955 as we turned twelve and eight respectively. My father never told us that we were moving overseas to Beirut, Lebanon, where he would be in charge of the Near East Regional Service Center (NERSC), which produced and distributed American propaganda throughout the Middle East and parts of North Africa. He was to supervise over ninety people of different nationalities. He had diplomatic status.

I had to guess that a move overseas was in the works from the fact that I was getting vaccinations and a passport and hearing snatches of conversation about going overseas between my father and others. Strangely enough it did not occur to me to ask questions. I nevertheless thought of it as an exciting prospect. I had finished elementary school and would have been going into junior high that fall, so I would be changing schools and losing friends anyway.

I of course expected Christine and Louis to come with us, and so did they. It came as a great shock to them and to us kids that my father all of a sudden decided to get married to one of his former office assistants. Now newly divorced, he perhaps felt it more appropriate as a diplomat to be accompanied by a wife rather than a sister and father. He must have thought he was in love, wanted a sex life once again, and hoped to establish a conventional family life. The latter never happened and the first faded.

There was little time between our learning about our prospective stepmother, the wedding, and our going off to Beirut. I had met her once before at my father's office and thought her lively and attractive. The only outing with her that I remember before the marriage was at the zoo and her asking me if I knew about menstruation. She seemed at the time very comforting, and I felt able to ask her about a vaginal discharge I had. She reassured me it was nothing to worry about. So our relationship started off at least on a friendly basis. As she had short hair, I even had my hair cut short to be like her.

Ricky and I saw our mother and grandmother briefly before going overseas. That on top of the divorce must have been hard for her as she would have realized in a very concrete way that she no longer had any say in what we did. The wedding took place on June 6, 1955, and immediately afterward, our father and stepmother drove to New York City for a honeymoon night. My father's best friend and his two sons drove Ricky and me there.

In New York, we met with our father and stepmother and boarded an ocean liner bound for Beirut. Christine and Louis, who had cared for us so much and for so long, were not even there to see us off. For the next few years, they were to play a very small role in Ricky's and my lives.

Life in Beirut was a far cry from life in Dubuque or Hyattsville. We lived in a huge apartment with four bed-rooms, three bath-rooms, and a maid's quarters. We had a cook, a live-in maid, and a cleaning woman, so our stepmother was freed from household chores, but in diplo-matic circles, there was a lot of socializing, and she was insecure and rather stiff in large so-cial settings.

In their letters she and my father continually complained to Christine and Louis about the obligatory social schedule they were expected to follow. They were often off to dinners and cocktail parties several nights a week and had to throw parties themselves including one for the US ambassador to Lebanon. Ricky and I actually enjoyed having the apartment to ourselves in the evenings. The maid usually stayed in her room. We would do silly things; Ricky would fill his wagon with stuffed animals and ride it down the long hallway throwing them at me as he passed my room.

In addition to the nighttime social events, my stepmother was expected to get involved in the Women's Club. There at least she found a position she liked. She became publicity chair, which involved using her writing skills, something she was good at and loved. She had in fact been promoted just before her marriage to my father and in the recommendation, she was commended for her contributions to various publications put out by the department. In a rare instance of her confiding to me, she expressed disappointment at the fact that despite my father's talking before the marriage of their writing articles together that never happened.

But soon, our relationship, which had started out well, turned sour. Ricky and I date it to her father's death. As mentioned earlier, he had died shortly after we arrived in Beirut, and at my father's insistence, she did not return for the funeral. Our stepmother was never quite the same after that.

She did not actually neglect us; she threw birthday parties for us and shepherded us to the beach, but she never made Ricky and me feel that she accepted and loved us. She exuded no warmth or ever seemed happy to have us around. We did not fight; we just coexisted. I cannot recall her ever kissing me. When the news arrived of her father's death, Ricky ran to her to try to give her a hug, but she pushed him away, ran into the bedroom, and slammed the door.

Ricky and I were in fact aliens to her, the children of another woman who had been married to our father, a fact that seemed to eat at her more as time went on. My mother's presence was felt of course because Ricky and I received letters and packages from her and Nana and we wrote to them as well. The piano we had had been my mother's. Years later, to my surprise, my stepmother complained about not being able to play the piano in Beirut. When I told her of course she could have played it, she said she had not felt welcome to do that.

There were many ironies to our situation in Beirut. One involved my brother's hair. For all the tension the length of my brother's hair had caused early on between my mother and father, neither my stepmother nor my father seemed initially at least to take responsibility for his getting haircuts, with the result that he earned the nickname "mop top" at school.

In addition, my mother at the top of her game would have been a real asset and thrived in the social world of Beirut, which my stepmother did not. Much as my mother had drunk up what Chicago had to offer when she was in her twenties, I relished the opportunity to observe and experience a different world. I was much involved in schoolwork and had friends at the small American Community School. My teachers there were generally stellar. The art teacher was the first nonrelative to tell me I had talent—like my mother. The gym teacher introduced me to many sports including the discus, javelin, high jumping, and basketball. I played on the varsity volleyball team.

The kids in my small class did a lot of socializing among ourselves, having parties and sleepovers, visiting each other's houses, drooling over Elvis, and so on. I was out of the house a lot, and to my father's credit, he let me be on my own on the streets in our neighborhood. I even took communal taxis downtown. At the time, most American parents there did not give their daughters such freedom.

During the first few years in Beirut, I was closer to my father than ever before or since. I got to do many things with him, but following his interests, not mine. Sometimes, we were all involved as a family group such as going on picnics in the mountains outside Beirut, and sometimes, I was just a tagalong as my stepmother apparently was not interested in accompanying him.

First picnic

My father loved history, which fueled my interest in the subject, and we would go on expeditions on the weekends to ancient cities including Tyre, Sidon, Byblos, and Baalbek as well as digging in Roman ruins near the Beirut airport. We visited Damascus several times and Jerusalem. He even got special permission to visit the famous Krak des Chevaliers that had been built on a mountaintop by the Knights Hospitaller with a two-thousand-strong garrison. It was huge with many round turrets and a spectacularly steep wall on one side that plunged into the valley below.

Church of the Nativity in what was then East Jerusalem

I also accompanied my father on his forays to a local jeweler where we would sit over Arabic coffee and make small talk before getting down to the purchase of items the jeweler had bought from Bedouins. We would visit an antique shop that had small Hellenistic sculptures my father purchased.

I even went with my father to what counted as a golf course in Beirut. My stepmother tried taking a few lessons from the local pro but gave up on it. The course was sand with only the putting greens actually being grass. Arabs would ride their beautiful Arabian horses through the course, and goat herders would wander by with their herds. I remember my father having an amicable exchange on the course with one herder, who enjoyed the cigarette my father offered him. Bill Blatty, who worked for my father and later wrote *The Exorcist*, used this incident in one of his humorous magazine pieces.

My father included me in a special interview he had with a State Department official who had escaped Iraq in the wake of the coup d'état in 1958 which had toppled the British-backed monarchy. My father had invited him to our apartment to talk despite the fact that my stepmother refused to remain in the house while the man, an African-American, was there. I sat on the floor while my father and the official talked, and I learned how he had escaped death by hiding under the bed at his hotel and not answering knocks on his door.

During all this time, I corresponded with my mother, grandmother, Christine, and my grandfather, all of whom kept my letters. I was never told not to write about certain things except for when I had bedbugs in the wooden bed loaned us by our landlord until our own furniture arrived. When the infestation was discovered, my father just said I would have to continue sleeping in the bed for a while, but I would have nothing to do with that as bedbug bites itch something terrible. I took over the sofa we had in the study.

As I have reread my letters home in preparation for writing this book, I noticed three things. All must have been instinctual as I made no conscious decision to write as I had. First, I made absolutely no mention of my stepmother and only a few references to "Daddy." Otherwise, I would just use "we." Second, I never wrote about what my father and I did on our own. Third, my letters were often rather long and detailed. It was as if I were creating this separate world of Ricky and myself to share with them.

Aug 3, 1955

Dear Christine and Grandpa,

We all got our letters and enjoyed them very much

Our days and nights here are very cool and sometimes are very windy. Some days the doors slam shut, so we have little pieces of wood we stick under them to keep them open.

We sometimes go shopping in the Soucks (which means "streets") where they have open markets. I will send you a post card of one. The stores here when are shut up (closed) look like garages (like this) [drawing]. Most of the stores are closed between 1 and 3 which is the hottest part of the day.

I have a piano teacher who comes twice a week and charges 2 and a half lb: a lesson (less than a dollar). But we haven't found a clarinet teacher yet.

Beirut Daddy says is much more modern then when he was here. It has lots of stores and a lot of apt. They are

2

They have two types of taxis here. One is one like at home and the others are called "services" which cost 25 piastres (about 7½¢) to take you anywhere on its route. It has a certian route on which it goes and are apt is on a street where it goes. You can tell them by their red license plates I better tell you the money exchange so I won't have to tell you each time. It is 3 ₤ for L.L and about 20 to 25 piastres to an American dollars the exchange rate changes everyday in piastres so that why I said 20 to 25. To find out what it is in American money divide the amount in Lebanonise (I don't think you spell it that way) by 3 and thats your answer.

Daddy is selling the white furniture and is going to get me some new furniture, Now that are furniture is here.

They have a USIS libary here and we belong to it and get alot of books from it.

I Love you a bushel and a peck! and a hug around the neck! Miss you

P.S. Say hello for me to the Bea—adriess

Love and kisses
Roberta

X X X X X X X X X X X X X X X X X X
X X X X X X X X X X X X X X X X X X

An early letter to my aunt and grandfather

I regularly reported my grades in school and wrote very enthusiastically about my activities. To my mother and Nana I wrote,

244

I am doing well in both my piano and clarinet. I had my piano recital not long ago and only made one mistake. I was sort of scared since this was my very first recital but I went through with it. I had such a long wait, it started with the very smallest up to the more advanced. I was 38th and very near the end of the LONG program. My music teacher's daughter played at least a 15 or 20 min. piece of Bach (which I think was boring and dull, since almost the whole piece was just fast scales).

A couple of days ago the "Rainy Season" started. It was not like I thought it would be. It rains for about a half an hour then the sun comes out and maybe for 2 hours it doesn't rain. Then it starts again. Of course it is only the beginning. It may rain longer then [sic] it does now.

I am sending a couple of pictures of the Garden of Gethsemane which I took while in Jerusalem. And also one of the Mt. of Olives also which I took their [sic]. Also a picture of the entrance gate to the Old Jerusalem where you go to get on to "Via Dolorosa" (or Street of Sorrow) where Jesus walked to his Crucifixion.

They have two types of taxis here, one is a regular and the other is called a service which carries more than one person it stoppes [sic] and picks up a lot of different people. It has a route which it travels and it cost 25 peastres [sic] (about 7 ½ cents).

On an Easter card sent to my mother, I wrote,

> Dear Mom, Guess whose [*sic*] a tennis fiend
> now? Me!!!! Barry McKay [an American
> professional tennis player] is here now and I go
> to see him play. I won the Tennis Doubles with
> my partner. So you see I'm going all out for it.
> Now that it's vacation time I'll have plenty of
> time for it.

In the summer of 1957, when I was fourteen, we returned to the United States for several months. At least at that time in the State Department, a tour of duty overseas lasted two years and then you had to come back, I suppose to re-Americanize.

My father allotted us only one week in August to be with our mother and grandmother, and I do not remember spending much time at all with Christine and Louis. They had left Hyattsville and returned to the house Christine owned in Chicago.

Despite Christine's earlier expectation that she had lost her opportunity to be head reference librarian at the University of Chicago when she left the assistant position to look after her mother ten years previously, she had not. When her mentor retired in 1957, she recommended Christine for the position, which must have been most gratifying to her. It was a coveted position in her field, and she remained there until retirement.

Until researching family documents for this book, I had thought it was the assistant position at the University of Chicago that Christine had given up to look after Ricky and me and felt somewhat guilty about that. So it was doubly gratifying to me that she had gotten what her good heart had desired and her professionalism deserved.

My mother had informed us that she was going to remarry; she and her fiancé picked Ricky and me up at Christine's home in Chicago and drove to Dubuque in his convertible. I did not take to him much; he seemed like a blowhard. The wedding never took place as the Catholic Church, despite the fact it had never blessed my mother's and father's marriage, regarded my mother as still married. The marriages of baptized Protestants were recognized by the Church. Aware of that, my father wrote a letter that he thought might be helpful by saying that he was not sure he had been baptized. But it was to no avail.

At that time, my mother was working at the lunch counter at Kresge's dime store, which many such establishments still had at that time. But Kresge's was a far cry from the Camellia House at the Drake and even from the Walgreen's in which my mother first started. Lobotomy or no lobotomy, she still was able to use her waitressing skills. She never seemed unhappy about it and never complained to me or my brother about what might have been.

In the fall of 1957, we were back in Beirut. I was fourteen and in the ninth grade. In the spring of 1958, however, sectarian strife broke out in Beirut. Lebanon was an artificial state that had been created by France after World War I and whose borders were deliberately established to give the Maronite Christians, a self-governing sect of Eastern Christianity, a slight majority over the Muslim population. Only in 1943 did it finally gain its independence. The constitution provided for the president to be Christian and the prime minister to be Muslim. The contrast between the two religious groups could not have been more dramatic than at the beach, where Muslim women draped in their black burkas took off their shoes and tentatively waded in the waves rolling in while the more sophisticated Christian women sunbathed in scanty bikinis.

The crisis was triggered by the kidnapping and assassination of a newspaper editor. The kidnapping took place just a few blocks from our apartment. In protest, a coalition Christian group in Beirut called for a general strike, and the opposition party, which was composed of Muslims, provoked riots to try to break the strike. My father was in fact in the thick of it. He wrote to Christine and Louis,

> Things got very violent day before yesterday. There was a pitched battle between Moslems trying to break the strike and the Christians, with the Government security forces coming in to halt the "festivities." Reliable reports say 35 to 50 were killed and several hundred wounded. I was down at NERSC on the day this happened, and in coming back home through town, I happened along at the time the trouble really got started. People were running for cover and shots were being fired in all directions. Two policemen jumped into my car and rode with me to the Embassy—they didn't want any part of it.

The central issue in the conflict in Lebanon was that Syrians were infiltrating the country to try to increase the number of Muslims and thus gain more power to force Lebanon to join the short-lived United Arab Republic Jamal Nasser of Egypt had formed with Syria in his bid to promote pan-Arabism. My letter to my mother and my grandmother on the situation shows excitement but little fear.

> I guess you've read about the exciting time we're having over here. For a while things were a little dangerous but lately everything is quieting down and getting back to normal. There are only a few bombs and some shooting going on. The Lebanese Army sure is doing a good job of cleaning things up. You see soldiers all over the place.
>
> The first week of the strike we had some excitement in our neighborhood. [We lived in an apartment building in which the owner, a minister in the Lebanese cabinet, also lived. When his car would pull up in front it was full of bodyguards conspicuously armed.] School was closed so all we did was watch out the balconys [*sic*] or listen to the radio. Well first of all in the back of our apartment someone put up a road block which brought a whole mass of soldiers to our area. Next, right across a vacant lot in back they found some Syrians hiding out as workmen in a new apartment building going up. They had a curfew at 8:00 (and still do) so

Ricky and I would watch the soldiers check the cars out front.

The 2nd week school started again from 8:00 to 1:00 straight. We had to go and return in cars. We were going to go to school on Saturday to make up for the lost time. But our principal Dr. Schutz received a note written in Arabic from the Opposition saying they hoped the school was "in sympathy with the opposition." Not knowing whether a crank had written it or not he decided to close the school ... We get full credits and no final exams ... It's rather boring now because I can't go to the movies or any place where there are big crowds except the beach [actually it was a beach club with a swimming pool]. I can't even go very far out of our apartment alone. So all I do is read or listen to the radio.

Please write because we haven't gotten any mail in a long time and we always look forward to news from home especially now.

I unfortunately did not keep my mother's and grandmother's letters, so I do not know what their reaction was or what they were reading in the newspapers. Nor do I know if my father sent them any kind of reassurance, but I assume he did.

Chapter 22

Rome and Our Return to the States

There was no talk of our leaving Beirut until the coup took place in Iraq and President Eisenhower sent the Marines to Lebanon at the request of that country's president. In July 1958, the ambassador ordered all American dependents to leave the city.

US warships in the harbor in Beirut

Ricky, my stepmother, and I went off as "refugees" to Rome. We stayed at a *pensione* near the Villa Borghese, and my exploring instincts immediately took hold. My stepmother wanted to move with other families to the outskirts of Rome, a move she thought would be beneficial particularly for Ricky. And she was right. We were in one large bedroom with three beds and ate in the dining room. Laundry facilities consisted of our bathtub. I still remember my brother's smelly socks tossed between our beds. But I wanted to stay where we were, which was far more central to all the interesting places in Rome. I

The Roman Forum

was totally adamant and selfish in my opposition. So we stayed. Why I was not overruled I do not know. If my stepmother had put her foot down and said we were moving, I would have moved. I had no idea she was suffering from what turned out to be a serious stomach complaint. She never showed any outward symptoms or told me.

My father was able to take a two-week vacation during the summer, and we drove through Europe in a little rented Fiat at a whirlwind pace. We stopped at Florence and Venice, then Innsbruck, Zurich, Frankfort, Cologne, and Brussels, where we visited the World's Fair. We returned via Reims, Geneva, and Leghorn in Italy. It was wonderful to see so much even in so short a time. Ricky and I ran up the stairs in the Tower of Pisa as well as in the Cologne Cathedral where suddenly we were thrust out on a metal grid that looked far down on the street below. I date my fear of heights from that experience.

Despite its being a fun trip, tensions lay underneath. I was becoming a teenager and moving emotionally away from my father. I was sensitive to and irked by his continual expectation that I just suck it up and fall in line with his wishes. Added to that was my stepmother's hostility, which came out directly for the first time during the trip. Charm bracelets were all the rage at the time, and I had been collecting charms for a while one at a time from countries we visited; I bought them with money my mother had sent me.

At one of our stops, I asked to go into a store to purchase a charm; my stepmother became very agitated and angry and told my father that she should have a charm bracelet too. He bought her one with many charms already on it. In retrospect I am not sure whether she envied me or was upset with my father's controlling the money or both. She was certainly unhappy.

My father also had another episode of expecting me to forgo my needs for the sake of his. At one point, we stayed at a hotel in France—all four of us in one room to save money. The omelet I had had for dinner sat in my stomach like a huge stone the whole night. The next morning, I was nauseous, but my father just packed me in the car and drove on. He stopped once to let me out of the car to vomit.

We arrived at a place for lunch, and I immediately went to the bathroom, which consisted of a hole in the floor. I had such bad cramps and diarrhea that I actually prayed to die. When I came back, I could only rest my head on the table. The proprietor was so concerned—not my father or stepmother—that he brought me some bicarbonate of soda, which immediately helped. I had expected some sympathy from my father because he had himself suffered ptomaine poisoning earlier in Beirut and had nearly died, but I was supposed to just carry on so we could meet his schedule.

My father returned to Beirut, and Ricky, my stepmother, and I to Rome, where I started to attend tenth grade at the Overseas School of Rome. Then another of my father's mercurial decisions occurred. In September, despite the fact he had been writing letters urging Christine and Louis to come to Beirut for a visit, he decided to leave government service. For someone who had been so ambitious in his earlier years and who had steadily moved up the career ladder, it was all the more striking. His job was demanding; he wrote to Christine, "I have never had a job with more pressure and problems, administrative and personnel." So perhaps the gild was off the lily and he had just burned out. He certainly faced more danger from the political turmoil in Lebanon than other embassy personnel did.

To be as inconspicuous as possible, NERSC was located across town, and my father had to pass through disputed areas in his commute. He once had to go up in the mountains to get some of his Lebanese workers past a roadblock. He described to me the angry mob banging on the car. Less serious but still a significant consideration was that he and my stepmother disliked the amount of time they had to spend socializing.

His best friend in the United States had left the State Department and was working in a business owned by his mother-in-law. He offered my father the position of assistant sales manager of her company in Long Island City, New York, and my father accepted in part because he felt at his age—he was nearing forty—he would not have a lot of job opportunities come his way.

So my father packed up our things in Beirut. We met him in Italy, and we sailed to New York and a house in the suburb of New Rochelle. His final evaluation as he left the government was excellent.

> The officer has effectively demonstrated his executive ability as Director of NERSC during unusually difficult political situations. His advance planning has made possible a smooth and effective integration of NERSC facilities with military information operation for which he has been commended by the Director of the Agency.

The director of the agency was the famous newsman Edward R. Murrow, who had been a prominent broadcaster during World War II and who had had the guts to confront McCarthy during his witch hunt for Communists in the government. The landing of the Marines was a surprise to American government personnel in Beirut. My father spearheaded the effort to assure the Lebanese populace of our friendly intent by writing the copy, arranging the printing, and helping coordinate air drops of leaflets in short order. It was his finest hour.

Ricky and I again attended new schools and had to make new friends, which we did. We would visit our mother and grandmother in Dubuque every summer again, often going on picnics to the magnificent Eagle Point Park on a bluff overlooking the Mississippi River and making trips to the Wisconsin Dells to stay in cabins at a resort with a beautiful sandy beach. The Dells was not quite as built up as it is today, but there was still plenty to do and see such as the Tommy Bartlett water skiing show, and we all had fun.

My mother and I never had mother-daughter talks and confidences; that tie had been broken, and such intimacy could not be resurrected in a few short weeks, but that does not mean we did not enjoy each other's company.

Meanwhile back in New Rochelle, my relationship with my father and stepmother continued to become more tense. My father was not around much as he worked on Long Island, which was a fair commute, and he often had to visit the plant in Camden, New Jersey. My stepmother became locked into the housewife role. There was only one car, which my father monopolized. As had been the case with my mother in

Hyattsville, my stepmother's movements were restricted, and so she was isolated. I do not think she made any friends. We lived near my father's best friend, but my stepmother never seemed comfortable around his wife.

My stepmother took a lot of her unhappiness out on me. She decided that ironing should be among the chores I should do to help around the house. Ironing was one of the most arduous household tasks of all—no permanent press in those days—and she knew I knew that. While visiting her mother after our first two-year tour of duty, she had talked about how ironing had been so backbreaking for her mother that her father had purchased a presser. I was determined not to let my stepmother win. I did the ironing including sheets and my father's dress shirts in a room over the garage with a television. While ironing, I watched many Mobile Theater TV shows with Zero Mostel in *Waiting for Godot*, Jason Robarts Junior in *The Iceman Cometh*, and Helen Hayes in *The Cherry Orchard*.

My stepmother had become pregnant within a few months of our return, so in addition to doing the ironing, I had to look after my sister after school. I actually enjoyed plopping my sister in a stroller and wandering the neighborhood while we giggled. But my stepmother did not entirely welcome the birth; she most likely suffered from

postpartum depression. When my sister was first home and would cry in the evenings, my stepmother thought the baby did not like her. My twelve-year-old brother, whose bedroom was nearest our sister's, would rock her to sleep.

My stepmother embarrassed me greatly when the mother of a friend came to call selling Avon products. She was angry and practically slammed the door in the women's face. Her anger certainly built up, and one night when we kids were upstairs, she and my father had a major row. It ended with my stepmother's leaving the house with a very definitive slamming of the door. My brother recalls her returning later and hearing some discussion about staying together for the sake of us kids.

In summers, my stepmother would take my sister and go off for weeks to her mother's house in Cumberland, Maryland. I was left with the housecleaning chores and cooking, which I fulfilled adequately given the circumstances and the fact that I received no help from the males in the family. My father liked mashed potatoes every night—real mashed potatoes— and that was the biggest task. I had to mash by hand; there were no Cuisinarts back then.

My brother and I grew particularly close at this time; he would come to my room, and I would read *Huckleberry Finn* to him. Both of us would roll on the floor laughing. It was good to have him around. We still share a peculiar sense of humor about our mutual past.

I also became much more politically active as the friends I had made were. My father even paid for my bus ticket for a march on Washington for civil rights in 1960 just a few short years before the march at which Dr. Martin Luther King Jr. gave his famous speech.

I also participated in a protest against air-raid drills. That was the age of paranoia about the nuclear bomb, and the schools were supposed to have air-raid drills. Others and I thought that ridiculous as we were just a few miles from a main target, New York City, and crouching in a corridor with our hands over our heads was not going to save us; it just gave a false sense of security that we felt was dangerous. If my parents were called about my refusal to participate in the drill, I never heard about it.

My actual withdrawal from my family occurred during my first year of college. The summer before my freshman year, my father quit his job and purchased the weekly newspaper in a small town in upstate New York about an hour from Cornell University, where I was headed. As I related earlier, to get money to help finance his purchase of the newspaper, he borrowed from his government pension and without my knowledge raided my bank account for the money I had earned working during the summer at a hospital.

When we moved that summer, Ricky and I were expected to work unpaid in the newspaper office. I proofed galleys, helped people order wedding invitations, and kept the books, which were checked by an accountant once a month. My stepmother stayed home to look after my sister. Thinking back on it, I do not see why they did not recruit me to babysit so my stepmother, who could write, could work alongside my father in the office.

I did well at Cornell, but I was not happy there. My small New York State Regents scholarship was the only spending money I had; I received nothing extra from my father, who of course was paying my tuition. My unhappiness stemmed mainly from the extreme isolation of the university on its own high hill, the lack of interest in the student body in political issues I thought important, and the dominance of the campus by the sorority and fraternity system.

I had almost no contact with my family. No one called or offered to pick me up and bring me home for a dinner. True, I did not call them, and in fact I went back to New Rochelle for Thanksgiving with my roommate with whom I had attended high school to see friends and watch the annual Thanksgiving Day football game at my former high school. I even in fact forgot my father's birthday, which was in November, a fact he pointed out to me with annoyance.

It was as if there were a vacuum. When I returned home for Christmas break, something happened that convinced me I did not want to remain in my father's home anymore. My father, Ricky, my sister, and I were out Christmas shopping in a nearby large town. My sister was holding my hand, and we were walking in front having a good time. She told me, "You know I love you more than I love my mother." My father immediately yelled in a loud, harsh voice, "No you don't!" I knew definitively that I was not really wanted as part of that household; I was too much of a disruptive presence.

Unlike my father when he was ten, I could leave and I had somewhere to go. So I left feeling independent and in control of my life. But in the process, I lost a father just as I had so many years before lost a mother. Our relationship was never the same as it had been in Beirut.

Chapter 23

Back to Chicago and Christine

The spring of my freshman year in college, Christine called to say that my grandfather Louis had died. She had moved from the south suburbs of Chicago to a small house near the University of Chicago. I do not remember how it all worked out, but I decided to take a leave of absence from Cornell, move in with Christine, and get a job in Chicago.

She had a small English basement apartment—one room and bath—that she offered to me, and I gladly accepted it. My father was a little uncertain about the wisdom of my leaving school, but I assured him I would complete my education. I knew my tuition was a big expense for him, so my going off to earn money must have been a relief. In fact, I understood that whoever controlled the purse strings had the right to make certain decisions in a person's life, and I wanted to be totally independent of my father. Before going, however, I had one more stint of having to take care of the house while my stepmother went with my sister to visit her folks in Maryland. I also worked in the newspaper office unpaid.

When I went to Chicago that fall, I felt guilty about leaving Ricky and my sister behind, but I knew there was little I could do about that. Even if I had stayed around when I was not attending college, I could not have protected them from the dysfunctional morass that existed. My father was a nice guy, very friendly to everyone, energetic, and full of ideas, but he was very self-absorbed and totally devoted to his work. My stepmother was just plain miserable in the role she had to play, and she made life miserable for those around her.

Once in Chicago, I entered Christine's calm, caring, and interesting world once again. She let me stay rent-free, but we shared grocery expenses. She gave me $100 to fix up the English basement, which had its own access, and she paid for a season of opera at the Lyric Opera. She loved opera and ballet, and I had fallen in love with opera after having seen *Carmen* at the Civic Opera House in Beirut with a traveling Italian company and *La Bohème* in Rome. The highlight of the season in Chicago was seeing Rudolph Nureyev, who had just defected from the Soviet Union, dance in *Boris Godunov*. He was stunning. A few years later when he was traveling the country with Lynn Fontaine as his dance partner, I bought Christine and me tickets to a performance in Chicago; that was a thrill.

I got a job as a secretary at the University of Chicago and saved almost every dime of my pay for my future tuition. My father had insisted that I take typing in summer school before I turned sixteen and could work during the summers. He pointed out that it would give me some skill "to fall back on." It was good foresight. As a full-time employee at the university,

I could take a course at half tuition, so I got permission from my boss to take a course offered late in the day—Russian Civilization—to see whether I liked studying there any better than I had at Cornell. I did, and when I applied, the admissions department resurrected my application from two years earlier and admitted me as a self-supporting, independent student.

The University of Chicago was one of the few institutions of higher learning at the time that accepted transfer students. As I would be paying my own way, my father did not have to pay a dime. Nor did he offer to. I was lucky enough to get a tuition scholarship for my last two years, and I worked twenty hours a week to pay for food and a roof over my head during those years.

Something wonderful came into Christine's life at that time; she became reacquainted with a man she had known in earlier days when she had boarded at his mother's house when she first worked at the University of Chicago. The family had been quite prominent in Chicago social life as his father had been vice president of the Illinois Central Railroad. But after the death of his father, the family fell on hard financial times, thus his mother's taking in boarders.

Gilbert had been quite the man about town, very handsome and artistic, going out with six different women in one day and paying little attention to Christine at the time. But then he started courting her, and they were soon married.

He changed her life. He took her on trips to a private island in Hawaii owned by a friend, to the Caribbean, and throughout Europe including a trip on the Orient Express.

Though he was an alcoholic, he fought it in any way he could, and Christine was accepting of him.

I moved into a studio apartment on my own, and Christine moved into the family home near the University of Chicago. My brother and I and subsequently our spouses and kids visited regularly and enjoyed the films Gilbert had shot of their trips with recorded music he had chosen in the background.

I made at least one trip back to New York for Christmas while I was an undergraduate at the university, but that was the last Christmas I spent there. Sometime later, after putting so much blood, sweat, and tears into modernizing the printing of the newspaper and forming a partnership with another weekly publisher to pool resources, my father visited New Mexico with my stepmother and sister and impulsively decided to purchase two motels there. He returned, sold his interest in the newspaper to his partner, and moved with whatever could be stuffed in a trailer back to New Mexico. My brother was left to close up the house.

My father and I as well as my stepmother exchanged very upbeat letters and talked periodically on the phone, but I never visited New Mexico nor was I urged to do so. However, my brother and I regularly visited our mother and grandmother in Dubuque usually around Christmas and during the summer.

When I became engaged, my mother and grandmother threw a bridal shower for me in Dubuque, and my mother and her best friend had a grand time at the wedding. My stepmother came with my father, but she refused to allow my young sister to be my ring bearer, which of course disappointed me.

A few years later when my brother was getting married, my father called to ask if Ricky would take a monetary gift rather than he and my stepmother coming to the wedding. That was bizarre; my brother, hurt by the offer, refused.

Chapter 24

The Ends Come

Before he settled in New Mexico, my father had earlier tried to restart his career in the government. He was good friends with Tom Sorenson, brother of Ted Sorenson, Kennedy's right-hand man and at the time the deputy director of the USIA. When Murrow quit his position in 1964 just a few months after Kennedy's assassination and Johnson's assumption of the presidency, Tom arranged for my father to have an interview for the prestigious position. But the Johnson administration was not looking to employ people associated with the Kennedy administration. My father had apparently been oblivious to that; perhaps because of his excellent evaluation when he left government service, he had not prepared for the interview and was raked over the coals. That ended those aspirations.

But wherever my father found himself, he was always in the thick of things. In Truth or Consequences, New Mexico, he became director of the Chamber of Commerce. A year later, he started working on the local newspaper and did that for a few years. In 1976, he became director of the Geronimo Springs Museum and subsequently the economic development coordinator for the Southern Rio Grande Council of Governments. So he chose a world in which to live and contribute that was smaller than the State Department world would have been.

After my stepmother's death from lupus, he decided to live out in a trailer in a godforsaken area with no telephone and work on his novel about World War II. He did come to visit my brother's and my families in Chicago several times, but he never showed great interest in his five grandchildren, and they never really got to know him. He remained, however, his outward, optimistic self and ended up with a woman in El Paso, Texas, with whom he had a solid relationship. My brother and I visited them and were glad he had finally landed in good hands. He died suddenly of a heart attack in November 1996. He was buried with military honors at Fort Bliss National Cemetery in El Paso.

He had written over the course of the years several wills. With one of them he left an envelope addressed, To My Children. It contained a handwritten letter,

> To my dear children, A will is such a cold and formal document, so I am adding this personally. I love each of you very much. You are my proud(est) legacy to this world. I thank you for the happiness and the deep sense of well-being that you have given me. My wish is that you also receive in the same full measure the love and affection that you gave to me. Your Dad

From my journey of discovery I realize that my father had much unhappiness in his life, some self-afflicted, but nonetheless painful for that. I hope indeed that we did bring him some happiness.

My mother died much earlier, before there were any grandchildren. Besides my visiting her, she came several times to Chicago to visit me—once unfortunately unexpectedly when I was in college and preparing for my written comprehensive exams. My brother came to the rescue and spirited her away. Another time, she visited when I was already married, and while I was at work, she was adventurous enough to find out that the Special Olympics was taking place at the University of Chicago that year and saw it. She was also adventurous enough while at our apartment to consider going from one of the bedroom windows to the flat roof next door to sunbathe. Thank goodness she thought better of it.

Knowing what I now know, I regret I did not go with her on a vacation bus trip she had won, but I was still wary of being part of her world and saw the trip as a possible claustrophobic experience. I tried to add a little excitement to her life by taking her to the Field Museum, but it did not really seem to interest her. And one time in Dubuque, I took her and Nana to dinner at a new French restaurant where we had vichyssoise soup for a first course. Instead of finding it adventurous to have a cold soup, my mother thought it very strange and did not seem to enjoy it. No excitement, no glamor; those had been sliced from her life.

At the end, my mother too found someone to cherish her—the brother of her former dance teacher when she was a teenager. He was a lens maker and had been at Los Alamos in New Mexico for many years. He retired to Dubuque and got my mother interested in the local astronomy club for which he built a telescope. He was a kind and gentle man and so good to my mother. Like my father, she ended up in a much smaller world than she deserved; it was not, however, a world of her own choosing and was one with which she had to live for most of her life. She did so with grace and without bitterness.

When I visited my mother for Christmas in 1974, I noticed that she was falling asleep in her chair quite a bit. I was concerned and urged her to see a doctor. I soon learned that she had developed breast cancer but had kept it a secret until it had eaten a hole in her breast. I was thirty-one and pregnant with my first child. I was upset with her for not having taken care of herself sooner. She told me that she did not want to go to the Mayo Clinic, which was of course where her father had died.

She was sent home and received hospice care there, but she fell out of bed and broke bones in her arms; she was put back in the hospital. I was too far along in my pregnancy to visit, and to my shame, I was reluctant to call until my grandmother upbraided me rightly for my neglect. I was behaving just like my father when faced with an emotional crisis.

My mother died in March 1975 with my grandmother by her side. She told Nana that she was handing over the care of Ricky and me to her. She then turned to the wall and died. That was two days before I gave birth to my daughter. I was actually mad at her for not holding on long enough to know that she had a granddaughter. I could not of course attend the funeral, but unasked, Christine chose to go to represent me.

Max Witte had died in 1953, almost a year after my mother had been paroled from the Independence Mental Health Institute. His personal care and faith in her ability to survive outside the institution is to my mind responsible for her recovery.

As mentioned earlier, Walter Freeman remained a continual presence in my mother's life as he was in the lives of many of his patients. He died in 1972.

My brother and I continued to visit Dubuque to see my grandmother, and I called her once a week. She had put herself into a very caring nursing home, where she rooted for the Cubs, her favorite baseball team. She participated in a poetry writing class and occasionally tended tomato plants she planted. She kept her wits about her until the very end.

In 1986, she underwent surgery for a cataract, and my brother surprised her by being there to be with her. She was delighted with his visit and to be able to see again more clearly. Within a few days, however, she had a severe heart attack. She declined going to the hospital. She died at age ninety-eight. The priest read one of the poems she had written at her funeral.

I remained close to Christine until her death. She retired from the University of Chicago, and she and her husband moved to a house in Del Rey Beach, Florida, that his family had owned for years. Her husband suffered from Alzheimer's, and true to the type of person she was, she would not put him in a home but looked after him with the help of a caregiver who came once a week. She even asked the doctor how she would know when he died; the doctor said to put a mirror over his lips, just like in *King Lear*.

I worried some about her living alone after her husband's death particularly because of hurricanes, but she assured me she had a good plan of evacuation. I called her every week. She and I had a wonderful time driving down highway A1A to Key Largo, stopping for me to snorkel at John Pennecamp Park, and exploring the Everglades by car.

In 1985, she slipped and fell when taking a bath and was not rescued and taken to the hospital until the caregiver, who was by then just staying in one of the bedrooms periodically, came home. In describing it, Christine was very offhand and showed no concern at all.

When she returned to her Del Rey Beach house, however, we arranged for a caregiver. My daughter, who needed a job for the summer, was also there with her when she died suddenly of a heart attack just one year before my father died. She wanted no funeral service, but I, who was the executor of her estate, ignored that wish; such services are for the benefit of the living. I organized a memorial service for her at the University of Chicago in the chapel where she had been married. She was beloved in that community, and the university flew the flag at half-mast for her, a singular and well-deserved honor.

She wanted to be cremated and buried alongside her husband in a beautiful, old graveyard in Louisville, Kentucky. Ricky and I were the only ones in attendance to give thanks to her for the crucial role she had played in our lives. Without her, we would have been overwhelmed by all that happened to us as kids. Her life examined is a tribute to her clear-sighted goodness.

Epilogue

I of course have had a life after all the principal players from my childhood have died. I graduated from college and did graduate work first in education and then in history. I married a man who wanted an independent woman and was willing to share in raising our two children and doing household tasks.

It took me eight years, however, to finally agree to have children as I felt my childhood had not prepared me to be a mother. My husband and I remained married until his much-too-early death. Though as I described earlier, I dropped out of graduate school rather than face possible failure, I had a satisfying and successful career in education as a writer, editor, and administrator. And I met my modest goals as an artist; I showed my work around the country including several solo exhibitions. And I have had the joy of seeing my children grow up to have solid marriages and satisfying careers themselves.

Later in life, however, the traits I had developed to cope during my childhood proved inadequate, and I experienced the two periods of depression I described at the beginning of this book. Major depression is not just the blues; it is a serious clinical condition that makes even getting out of bed a seemingly impossible task. Dealing most effectively with it involves not only medication but also talking out concerns and issues with a professional who can provide much-needed support and perspective. Freeman did not believe that patients could benefit from insight.[93] That may be true for those with certain severe conditions, but it has certainly not been so in my case.

When I first thought of writing about my journey of understanding what happened and how I became who I was, I was hesitant. The media is so filled these days with images of gruesome atrocities and descriptions of the most terrible child abuse that can only be termed major tragedies; I thought my struggles were negligible in comparison to that. But I obviously changed my mind.

Although much mentioned, mental illness is still stigmatized and usually talked about only in generalities. Even William Styron's seminal *Darkness Visible*, discussing his own bout with depression, is in the end rather vague and not very helpful in regard to treatment. I wanted to change that. I had the materials to present a no-holds-barred look at mental illness. It does not develop overnight nor is it easily treated. In fact family members' attitudes and emotional states greatly affect, for better or worse, how it is treated. I wanted that to be very clear and to also offer hope that despite the horrendous toll mental illness takes, there is the possibility of recovery if a patient is surrounded by the right people.

Due to rising suicide rates and the use of alcohol, opiates, and other drugs to deal with the pervasive high levels of anxiety in this country, I thus felt it important to draw back the curtain from mental illness and face it frankly and honestly in the hope that this would encourage a deeper conversation and understanding of its nature and origins. Mental illness does not exist in a vacuum.

As stated at the beginning of the book, my personal goal was to put my memories of what happened in my childhood in some order. That I have done and more. There are still unanswered questions as there inevitably are about the past, but I no longer feel like a ricocheting ball in a pinball machine.

Most important, in the process, I learned a great deal about the origins of my strengths and vulnerabilities and in some instances their being one and the same. Knowing and accepting these I trust will help ward off further periods of depression. I know that I can be too independent and think that others find me just too much and a burden. I am learning to ask for help when I need it and to share much more of my time with friends and family.

I used to fantasize about living alone in some impregnable home built into a hillside. I do not do that anymore. I know that I am a caretaker by nature and sometimes put my own needs and desires aside for those of others. That is a good trait, but I tend to overdo it.

Not surprisingly and most especially, I have difficulty setting boundaries with other people and even with myself. I had so many people breaching my boundaries as a child to try to make me what they thought I should be that I am still most vulnerable in that area. Even during my period of research, I experienced a third depression over just such an issue. I know now to watch out for that.

The Romans had a saying (cribbed from the Greeks) *scitote*—know thyself. It is in the future imperative, a tense we do not have in English. It carries with it the idea of a continual self-examination. So I know I will need to look at my attitudes, emotions, and actions all my life.

I started this process by asking myself about my personal motives in writing this book, which after all is very revealing, personal, and in many ways upsetting. I must admit that there was a strain of getting even as part of the process at first, but I tried my best to pull back from any bitterness. My mother served as a good role model for that. I accept what I am and the cards I have been dealt, but I examine those cards carefully. I tried to keep people on the periphery of the story as anonymous as possible and to give as balanced an examination as I could of the lives of my mother, father, Nana, Pearl, and Christine.

Did these people or Freeman stop to examine why they had thought and acted as they had? From the information available to me, most did not really look very hard inside themselves. The consequences were harsh indeed. My mother lost the most—her sparkle and drive and a life with a husband and children. My mother's diary, poetry books, and scrapbooks were a revelation to my brother and me. We are so grateful that she at least had had that magical time in Chicago when she had great fun and great success. And we are grateful that she was able to live a relatively normal life with its own rewards and joys after her institutionalization.

My father was certainly not introspective. I once thought I knew him much better than I did my mother, but that is not the case now. I cannot fathom what led to his sanctioning the lobotomy and then dumping the responsibility for my mother on Nana. It was in many ways cowardly although he was not a coward as his actions in Beirut proved. I am glad that my father had custody of Ricks and me as it allowed us to have many more opportunities, and I am grateful for the support he gave me in being an independent individual whether it was due to benign neglect as my brother thinks or not. His failure, however, to recognize the effects of his mercurial changes of course, actions, and words on his children in the end made intimacy with him impossible for me.

Pearl was so bound up in her self-righteousness that she seemed unable to spare any real sympathy for me or my mother. I was a bad seed. She certainly did not understand or love me. That I had lost my mother and rarely saw my father did not cause her to stop and think about how I really felt; I was to conform to what she thought was presentable and proper. But she did care about my brother and at least examined her fitness for the job of caring for us. She is the reason Christine came into our lives.

I think my grandmother Nana had the pure instincts of a mother toward her child, but she certainly did not question her conventional views on the primacy of the husband in a marriage and the sexual mores of the time. She did not continence my mother's complaints about my father's not satisfying her sexually.

Christine was the most introspective of all. She was clear about her motives for her actions and navigated the personalities around her with considerable deftness and sensitivity. Despite the rejection of my mother by other family members, she never broke ties with her. The picture of the two of them at my wedding is one of joy.

In his unpublished autobiography, Freeman did some examination of his life. Most puzzling to interpret is the statement he made that his follow-up of his transorbital lobotomy patients was "an obsession, a hobby or an expiation, depending upon how one looked at lobotomy." He used the phrase "an obsession, a hobby or an expiation" twice in the work.[94] The term *expiation* is associated with sin. Did this man, who on his own count performed 3,500 lobotomies,[95] have regrets later in life? Were his head-and-shoulders hunting trips, as he called them in reference to his following up patients and taking their photographs, an effort to assure himself that he had done some good? He admitted, "It is easy to get lost in the frontal lobes, and sometimes with results ranging from the negligible to the disastrous."[96]

Certainly at the height of his career, however, he never seemed to question the rightness of the procedure he performed. He was egotistical. In the postcards and letter preserved by my grandmother, he wrote entirely of himself. He was not, however, some sort of Svengali. Although he could be seemingly nonchalant about what happened to patients during procedures, he did seem to care enough about my mother's condition to visit her, something my father did not. My grandmother certainly liked him. On the envelope in which she saved his postcards and letter, she wrote, "From Dr. Freeman who operated on Gretchen in Silver Springs, Maryland. He was very wonderful to us and tried to help Gretchen."

The lobotomy craze should not be considered an isolated event. Although there is now institutional review of experiments, the moral issue of weighing risks versus benefits remains very much a part of the conversation. There is considerable interest in electrical stimulation of specific areas of the brain to treat Parkinson's disease, depression,[97] and dementia, the latter significantly enough reported in a popularly circulated magazine, the *AARP Bulletin*.[98] Some clinics offer blood plasma infusion as a possible but unproven way of slowing down or stopping aging.[99] There has been an outburst of research and development on neurotechnology, the interface between brain and machine, that has produced for example the BrainGate System that has allowed an individual paralyzed from the shoulders up to feed himself via thoughts communicated through implants in his brain to electrodes in his arm muscles. As *The Economist* stated in reporting on this, "Beneath the skull lies the next frontier."[100] Freeman thought so too.

And in all this mix there still exist people desperate for help, medical personnel eager to make names for themselves, a media seeking stories about possible cures, and patients and governmental units looking for quick and inexpensive ways to deal with major health issues. This can and does for example lead to particular drugs being prescribed for and procedures being performed on patients based on those drugs' and procedures' popularity rather than on sound, researched medical reasons.[101]

Thus, it is even more imperative to question others, get solid information, and question yourself. Examine yourself and your motives not only when the decision affects yourself but most particularly when it affects someone else in your life. With an aging population, this will be an ever more frequent occurrence.

All of the people in this book thought they were doing good in their own eyes, but doing good is a slippery slope as it comes from our own attitudes, prejudices, and emotional states about what is best for someone else. Being kind is a condescending stance with the connotation of an adult patting a child on the head. I prefer doing kind—taking the time to understand the other person and what he or she is going through and act with kindness on that knowledge.

This is not easy certainly in regard to mental illness. Mental illness is something terrible; as I know too well, it can turn life into a living hell for an individual and those around him or her. It can, however, be faced and mitigated in the right circumstances particularly with the right people surrounding the individual.

In this book, I believe there were three people who were the right people doing kind at the right time: Nana, Witte, and Christine. While Nana was certainly uptight about sex, she stood by my mother, and she came to share Witte's optimism that my mother could leave the institution; she persevered along with Witte under some terrifying times. She is a model for standing by someone who is mentally ill when the temptation to back away is strong. She had her moments of doubt, but she was there for the long haul.

From the beginning, Witte and his staff worked to get my mother back into the world. His dogged patience and support along with the environment created by his staff eventually led to that goal; the role of mental institutions can be positive.

For Ricks and me, Christine was the right person. I cannot stress enough the importance of what someone so clear thinking, kind, and loving can do for kids facing stress and adversity. It is a role that can be played by anyone in regard to such children. Do kind.

Acknowledgments

I always read the acknowledgements in books. Trite as they sometimes seem, I know that writers do not function in bubbles, and although they are in the end responsible for the content of their works, they have had support and assistance in gathering, sifting, and processing information and in clarifying their emotional reactions to that information. I am of course no exception; I have many people to thank who helped me on the way.

First and foremost is my brother Richard Reb (Ricks to me), who not only lent me considerable emotional support but also supplied important information about our parents of which I was unaware; he did some of the spadework in obtaining access to important material on which this book is based. I cannot thank him enough.

Dennis Shelby, PhD, and Dr. Fred Shick went on this long journey of examining lives with me, asking important questions, and providing important insights.

The staff, particularly Leah Richardson in Special Collections of the Gelman Library at George Washington University, to which Walter Freeman donated his papers, were most helpful as was Dr. Bhasker J. Dave, superintendent of the Independence Mental Health Institute, and his staff members, particularly Keith Curry, who gave me a personal tour of the facility when I visited, and Mike Cook, who wrote a history of IMH and oversees the small museum they maintain.

As I learned in my research, medical institutions go out of existence or merge with others with the consequent loss of information about patients. That these two institutions respect and maintain historical records is certainly gratifying to a historian.

Contrary to what we have come to expect, not everything is on the internet. I spent long hours at the John Crerar Library, one of the best research libraries in the country in the fields of science, medicine, and technology, and at the Regenstein Library, both at the University of Chicago. My aunt had been head of reference services at Regenstein, and I was not hesitant in calling on the current reference staff for invaluable assistance.

My thanks also to Mark Allen, who provided me with legal advice as well as to the staff at the History of Medicine Division, Historical Library of Medicine, National Institutes of Health; John Michel; and Laura Feltzer-Vacek.

Special appreciation goes to Mario Aranda and Paul Fagen, friends indeed.

Endnotes

1   "Venereal Disease," in Paul Fass, ed., *Encyclopedia of Children and Childhood in History and Society*, Th-W (Gale, 2003), retrieved from faqs.org/childhood, September 18, 2017.

2   Fass, *Encyclopedia of Children*.

3   Private communication, History of Medicine Division, Historical Library of Medicine, National Institutes of Health, February 25, 2016.

4   There are a considerable number of studies of the effect of childhood sexual abuse; for example, Elizabeth Oddone Paolucci et al., "A Meta-Analysis of the Published Research on the Effects of Child Abuse," *The Journal of Psychology: Interdisciplinary and Applied* 135, no. 1 (2001): 17–36; Debra Neumann et al., "The Long-Term Sequelae of Childhood Sexual Abuse in Women: A Meta-Analytic Review," *Child Maltreatment* 1, no. 1 (February 1996): 6–16.

5   Susan E. Cutler and Susan Nolen-Hoeksema, "Accounting for Sex Differences in Depression through Female Victimization: Childhood Sexual Abuse," *Sex Roles* 24, nos. 7/8 (1991): 425.

6   Thomas C. Sorensen, *The Word War: The Story of American Propaganda* (New York: Harper & Row, 1968), 10.

7   See Jacqueline Wolf, *Deliver Me from Pain: Anesthesia and Birth in America* (Baltimore: John Hopkins University Press, 2009), 69, and Gladys Denny Schultz, "Journal Mothers Report on Cruelty in Maternity Wards," *Ladies Home Journal* LXXV, no. 5 (May 1958): 44–45, 152–55.

8   See for example Carole Kismaric and Marvin Heiferman, *Growing Up with Dick and Jane: Learning and Living the American Dream* (New York: Collins, 1996).

9   Alfred Henry Tyrer, *Sex Satisfaction and Happy Marriage* (New York: Emerson Books, 1963), 140. There were various unnumbered editions of this book going back to the late 1930s.

10   Schultz, "Journal Mothers Report," 44–45, 152–55.

11   Kinsey, *Sexual Behavior in the Human Female*, 12; William Masters and Virginia Johnson, *Human Sexual Response* (Boston: Little Brown, 1966), vi, 60.

12   Kinsey, *Sexual Behavior in the Human Female*, 132.

13   James Whorton, "The Solitary Vice," *Western Journal of Medicine* 175, no. 1 (July 2001): 66–68.

14   Walter Freeman, "Transorbital Lobotomy," *American Journal of Psychiatry* 108, no. 11: 824.

15   Walter Freeman, Unpublished autobiography, 1970 ca., box 9, folder 2, Walter Freeman and James Watts collection, MS0803 UA, Special Collections Research Center, George Washington University Libraries, chap. 3, p. 1.

16   Freeman, autobiography, chap. 13, pp. 2–3.

17   S. A. Wilson, "Occasional Notes: Report of the Conference of the Program—Executive Committee of the Second International Congress, London 1935," *The Journal of Neurology and Psychopathology* 55 (January 14, 1934): 283–88.

18   "International Neurological Conference in London," *The British Medical Journal* 2, no. 3891 (August 3, 1935): 223–25; no. 3892 (August 10, 1933): 269–72.

19   "Lobotomy," (last updated 12–17–2012), *Encyclopaedia Britannica*, retrieved from http://www.britannica.com, March 11, 2017.

20   Freeman, autobiography, chap. 16, p. 7.

21   Egas Moniz, *Tentatives Operatoires Dans le Traitement de Certaines Psychoses* (Paris: Masson & Cie., 1934), 194–210, my translation.

22   Thomas Ban, "Fifty Years Chlorpromazine: A Historical Perspective," *Neuropsychiatry, Disease and Treatment* 3, no. 4 (August 2007): 495–500.

23 "The Lobotomy Files: One Doctor's Legacy," Wall Street Journal Projects (2013), projects.wsj.com.

24 For example, the topectomy, which involved the actual removal of part of the cerebral cortex; Freeman, autobiography, chap. 14, p. 16.

25 Jon Harkness, abstract, "Nuremburg and Wartime Experiments on US Prisoners. The Green Committee," *Journal of the American Medical Association* 278, no. 20 (November 27, 1996): 1612–15, retrieved from https://www.ncbi.nim.nih.gov/pubmed/8922455 on May 23, 2016.

26 "U.S. Public Health Service Syphilis Study at Tuskegee: The Tuskegee Timeline," Centers for Disease Control and Prevention, https://www.cdc.gov>tuskegee>timeline.

27 Walter Freeman and James Watts, *Psychosurgery: Intelligence, Emotion and Social Behavior Following Prefrontal Lobotomy for Mental Disorders* (Springfield, IL: Charles C. Thomas, 1942), 79–84.

28 There has been widespread reporting of this incident; see for example Kate Clifford Larson, *Rosemary: The Hidden Kennedy Daughter* (New York: Houghton Mifflin Harcourt, 2015).

29 Freeman and Watts, Preface to *Psychosurgery*, 1st ed., i.

30 Ibid., 213.

31 Ibid., 208–9, 289, 302, 303, 312.

32 Ibid., 140, 143–44, 202.

33 "The Lobotomy Files: One Doctor's Legacy."

34 Freeman, autobiography, chap. 14, p. 7.

35 Ibid.

36 Ibid., chap. 9, p. 14.

37 "The Lobotomy Files: One Doctor's Legacy."

38 Walter Freeman, "Showmanship in Medical Teaching," *Journal of Medical Education* 28, no. 1 (January 1953): 31–35.

39 Freeman, autobiography, chap. 1, p. 3.

40 Ibid., chap. 5, p. 18; chap. 7, pp. 8A–9.

41 Ibid., chap. 5, p. 22.

42 Ibid., autobiography, chap. 14, p. 7.

43 Ibid., chap. 12, p. 7.

44 Elliot S. Valenstein, "A History of Lobotomy: A Cautionary Tale," *Michigan Quarterly Review* 27, no. 3(2): 430, retrieved from http://hdl.hanle.net/2027/;spo.act2080.0027.003:06 (April 2017).

45 Waldemar Kaempffert, "Turning the Mind Inside Out," *The Saturday Evening Post* 21 (May 24, 1941): 18–19, 69, 71–72, 74.

46 Gretchen J. Diefenbach, et al., "Portrayal of Lobotomy in the Popular Press: 1935–1960." *Journal of the History of the Neurosciences* 8, no. 1 (1999), 63–64.

47 Freeman, autobiography, chap. 14, pp. 12–13.

48 Ibid., chap. 14, p. 13.

49 "Biographical Note," Guide to the Walter Freeman and James Watts Collection, 1918–1988, Collection number MS0803.UA, https://library.gwu.edu/read/ms0803.xmi (April 28, 2017).

50 Freeman, autobiography, chap. 14, p. 12.

51 Walter Freeman and James Watts, *Psychosurgery: In the Treatment of Mental Disorders and Intractable Pain*, 2nd ed. (Springfield, IL: Charles C. Thomas, 1950), 358–59.

52 Walter Freeman, "Psychosurgery," *American Journal of Psychiatry* 114, no. 7 (1958): 608–9.

53 Walter Freeman et al, "The West Virginia Lobotomy Project," *Journal of the American Medical Association* 156, no. 10 (November 6, 1954): 939.

54 Elaine Showalter, *The Female Malady: Women, Madness, and English Culture, 1830–1980* (New York: Pantheon Books, 1985), 209.

55 Freeman, "The West Virginia Lobotomy Project," 940.

56 Freeman and Watts, *Psychosurgery*, 2nd edition, 531.

57 Ibid., 529.

58 Ibid., 119.

59 Ibid., 500.

60 Ibid., 183.

61 Ibid., 183.

62 Ibid., 511.

63 Ibid., 511–12.

64 Freeman, autobiography, chap. 2, p. 2.

65 Ibid., p. 3.

66 Ibid.

67 Ibid.

68 Freeman, autobiography, chap. 8, pp. 19–20.

69 Ibid., p. 20.

70 Freeman and Watts, *Psychosurgery* 2nd ed., 114.

71 Freeman, autobiography, chap. 12, p. 9.

72 Ibid., chap. 2, pp. 3–4.

73 Diefenbach, "Portrayal of Lobotomy in the Popular Press," 66.

74 "Lobotomy Disappointment," *Newsweek* 34 (December 12, 1949): 51.

75 "Personality Shifts Laid to Surgery," *New York Times* (December 14, 1947): 51; K. Goldstein, "Prefrontal Lobotomy: Analysis and Warning," *Scientific American* 182 (February 1950): 44–47; M. Gumpert, "Lobotomy: Savior or Destroyer?" *The Nation* 167 (November 6, 1948) 517–18.

76 Walter Freeman, "Ethics of Psychosurgery," *New England Journal of Medicine* 249, no. 20 (November 12, 1953): 798–801.

77 Ibid., 799.

78 Freeman, "Psychosurgery," *American Journal of Psychiatry*, 608–9.

79 Freeman, autobiography, chap. 21, pp. 3–4.

80 *The Early History of the Independence MHI: An introduction to the hospital's rich history and the "Days of Yore,"* the hospital's museum, compiled by Mike Cook, volunteer curator of the "Days of Yore." (Printed privately by the MHI Employee's Credit Union, 2012), 30.

81 Thomas Kirkbride, *On the Construction, Organization and General Arrangements of Hospitals for the Insane* (Philadelphia: B. Lippincott, 1880).

82 *The Early History,* 1.

83 Kirkbride, *On the Construction,* 23.

84 *The Early History,* 63, and private communication from IMH staff member during tour of the Institute.

85 Kirkbride, *On the Construction,* 264, 273.

86 *The Early History,* 52–53.

87 Ibid., 115–17.

88 Ibid., 103.

89 Harry Hamilton Laughlin, *Eugenical Sterilization in the United States* (Chicago: The Psychopathic Laboratory of the Municipal Court of Chicago, December, 1922), 1–2, 9.

90 https://wm.wikipedia/org.wiki/Eugenics_in_the_United_States, retrieved April 24, 2017.

91 Transcript for "The Lobotomist," PBS, The American Experience, ec2-184-73-243-168.compute-1.amazonaws.com. Also available at https://www.yumpo.com>view>the-lobotomist. The video of the program is available from PBS.

92 Freeman, autobiography, chap. 18, p. 4.

93 Ibid., chap. 14, p. 10.

94 Ibid., chap. 8, p. 17; chap. 14, p. 6.

95 Ibid., chap. 18, p. 19.

96 Ibid., chap. 14, p. 21.

97 Clyde Haberman, "The Quest for a Psychiatric Cure," April 16, 2017, mobile.nytimes.com.

98 "Jump-Starting the Brain's Memory," *AARP Bulletin*, 58, no. 6 (July–August 2017): 6.

99 "Youthful Spirits," *The Economist* (online subscription), July 15, 2017, Science and Technology, retrieved July 20, 2017.

100 "Neurotechnology: The Next Frontier" and "Thought Experiments," "Headache," "Inside Intelligence," "Translation Required," "Eberhard Fetz," and "Grey Matter, Red Tape" in the Technology Quarterly section, *The Economist* (online subscription), January 6, 2018, retrieved January 6, 2018.

101 Valenstein, "The History of Lobotomy," 430–37.

Printed in the United States
By Bookmasters